HENRY
OF
NAVARRE

HENRY OF NAVARRE

Albert C. Gross

CHELSEA HOUSE PUBLISHERS
NEW YORK
NEW HAVEN   PHILADELPHIA

EDITOR-IN-CHIEF: Nancy Toff
EXECUTIVE EDITOR: Remmel T. Nunn
MANAGING EDITOR: Karyn Gullen Browne
COPY CHIEF: Juliann Barbato
PICTURE EDITOR: Adrian G. Allen
ART DIRECTOR: Giannella Garrett
MANUFACTURING MANAGER: Gerald Levine

Staff for HENRY OF NAVARRE:

SENIOR EDITOR: John W. Selfridge
COPY EDITOR: James Guiry
EDITORIAL ASSISTANT: Sean Ginty
ASSOCIATE PICTURE EDITOR: Juliette Dickstein
PICTURE RESEARCHER: Lynne Goldberg
SENIOR DESIGNER: David Murray
ASSISTANT DESIGNER: Jill Goldreyer
PRODUCTION COORDINATOR: Joseph Romano
COVER ILLUSTRATION: Peter McCaffrey

CREATIVE DIRECTOR: Harold Steinberg

First Printing

1 3 5 7 9 8 6 4 2

Library of Congress Cataloging in Publication Data

Gross, Albert C.

Henry of Navarre/Albert C. Gross.
p. cm.—(World leaders past & present)
Summary: A biography of the French king who resolved religious conflict
in his country, issued the Edict of Nantes, and made other important
reforms before being assassinated.

ISBN 0-87754-531-6
1. Henry IV, King of France, 1553–1610— Juvenile
literature. 2. France— Kings and rulers—Biography—
Juvenile literature. 3. France—History—Henry IV,
1589–1610—Juvenile literature. [1. Henry IV, King of
France, 1553–1610. 2. Kings, queens, rulers, etc.
3. France—History—Henry IV, 1589–1610.] I. Title.
II. Series.
DC122.8.G76   1988   B
944'.031'0924—dc 19
[B]
[92] 87-26583 CIP AC

_____ Contents _____

WORLD LEADERS PAST & PRESENT

JOHN ADAMS
JOHN QUINCY ADAMS
KONRAD ADENAUER
ALEXANDER THE GREAT
SALVADOR ALLENDE
MARC ANTONY
CORAZON AQUINO
YASIR ARAFAT
KING ARTHUR
HAFEZ AL-ASSAD
KEMAL ATATÜRK
ATTILA
CLEMENT ATTLEE
AUGUSTUS CAESAR
MENACHEM BEGIN
DAVID BEN-GURION
OTTO VON BISMARCK
LÉON BLUM
SIMON BOLÍVAR
CESARE BORGIA
WILLY BRANDT
LEONID BREZHNEV
JULIUS CAESAR
JOHN CALVIN
JIMMY CARTER
FIDEL CASTRO
CATHERINE THE GREAT
CHARLEMAGNE
CHIANG KAI-SHEK
WINSTON CHURCHILL
GEORGES CLEMENCEAU
CLEOPATRA
CONSTANTINE THE GREAT
HERNÁN CORTÉS
OLIVER CROMWELL
GEORGES-JACQUES
  DANTON
JEFFERSON DAVIS
MOSHE DAYAN
CHARLES DE GAULLE
EAMON DE VALERA
EUGENE DEBS
DENG XIAOPING
BENJAMIN DISRAELI
ALEXANDER DUBČEK
FRANÇOIS & JEAN-CLAUDE
  DUVALIER
DWIGHT EISENHOWER
ELEANOR OF AQUITAINE
ELIZABETH I
FAISAL
FERDINAND & ISABELLA
FRANCISCO FRANCO
BENJAMIN FRANKLIN

FREDERICK THE GREAT
INDIRA GANDHI
MOHANDAS GANDHI
GIUSEPPE GARIBALDI
AMIN & BASHIR GEMAYEL
GENGHIS KHAN
WILLIAM GLADSTONE
MIKHAIL GORBACHEV
ULYSSES S. GRANT
ERNESTO "CHE" GUEVARA
TENZIN GYATSO
ALEXANDER HAMILTON
DAG HAMMARSKJÖLD
HENRY VIII
HENRY OF NAVARRE
PAUL VON HINDENBURG
HIROHITO
ADOLF HITLER
HO CHI MINH
KING HUSSEIN
IVAN THE TERRIBLE
ANDREW JACKSON
JAMES I
WOJCIECH JARUZELSKI
THOMAS JEFFERSON
JOAN OF ARC
POPE JOHN XXIII
POPE JOHN PAUL II
LYNDON JOHNSON
BENITO JUÁREZ
JOHN KENNEDY
ROBERT KENNEDY
JOMO KENYATTA
AYATOLLAH KHOMEINI
NIKITA KHRUSHCHEV
KIM IL SUNG
MARTIN LUTHER KING, JR.
HENRY KISSINGER
KUBLAI KHAN
LAFAYETTE
ROBERT E. LEE
VLADIMIR LENIN
ABRAHAM LINCOLN
DAVID LLOYD GEORGE
LOUIS XIV
MARTIN LUTHER
JUDAS MACCABEUS
JAMES MADISON
NELSON & WINNIE
  MANDELA
MAO ZEDONG
FERDINAND MARCOS
GEORGE MARSHALL

MARY, QUEEN OF SCOTS
TOMÁŚ MASARYK
GOLDA MEIR
KLEMENS VON METTERNICH
JAMES MONROE
HOSNI MUBARAK
ROBERT MUGABE
BENITO MUSSOLINI
NAPOLÉON BONAPARTE
GAMAL ABDEL NASSER
JAWAHARLAL NEHRU
NERO
NICHOLAS II
RICHARD NIXON
KWAME NKRUMAH
DANIEL ORTEGA
MOHAMMED REZA PAHLAVI
THOMAS PAINE
CHARLES STEWART
  PARNELL
PERICLES
JUAN PERÓN
PETER THE GREAT
POL POT
MUAMMAR EL-QADDAFI
RONALD REAGAN
CARDINAL RICHELIEU
MAXIMILIEN ROBESPIERRE
ELEANOR ROOSEVELT
FRANKLIN ROOSEVELT
THEODORE ROOSEVELT
ANWAR SADAT
HAILE SELASSIE
PRINCE SIHANOUK
JAN SMUTS
JOSEPH STALIN
SUKARNO
SUN YAT-SEN
TAMERLANE
MOTHER TERESA
MARGARET THATCHER
JOSIP BROZ TITO
TOUSSAINT L'OUVERTURE
LEON TROTSKY
PIERRE TRUDEAU
HARRY TRUMAN
QUEEN VICTORIA
LECH WALESA
GEORGE WASHINGTON
CHAIM WEIZMANN
WOODROW WILSON
XERXES
EMILIANO ZAPATA
ZHOU ENLAI

CHELSEA HOUSE PUBLISHERS

ON LEADERSHIP

Arthur M. Schlesinger, jr.

LEADERSHIP, it may be said, is really what makes the world go round. Love no doubt smooths the passage; but love is a private transaction between consenting adults. Leadership is a public transaction with history. The idea of leadership affirms the capacity of individuals to move, inspire, and mobilize masses of people so that they act together in pursuit of an end. Sometimes leadership serves good purposes, sometimes bad; but whether the end is benign or evil, great leaders are those men and women who leave their personal stamp on history.

Now, the very concept of leadership implies the proposition that individuals can make a difference. This proposition has never been universally accepted. From classical times to the present day, eminent thinkers have regarded individuals as no more than the agents and pawns of larger forces, whether the gods and goddesses of the ancient world or, in the modern era, race, class, nation, the dialectic, the will of the people, the spirit of the times, history itself. Against such forces, the individual dwindles into insignificance.

So contends the thesis of historical determinism. Tolstoy's great novel *War and Peace* offers a famous statement of the case. Why, Tolstoy asked, did millions of men in the Napoleonic Wars, denying their human feelings and their common sense, move back and forth across Europe slaughtering their fellows? "The war," Tolstoy answered, "was bound to happen simply because it was bound to happen." All prior history predetermined it. As for leaders, they, Tolstoy said, "are but the labels that serve to give a name to an end and, like labels, they have the least possible connection with the event." The greater the leader, "the more conspicuous the inevitability and the predestination of every act he commits." The leader, said Tolstoy, is "the slave of history."

Determinism takes many forms. Marxism is the determinism of class. Nazism the determinism of race. But the idea of men and women as the slaves of history runs athwart the deepest human instincts. Rigid determinism abolishes the idea of human freedom—

the assumption of free choice that underlies every move we make, every word we speak, every thought we think. It abolishes the idea of human responsibility, since it is manifestly unfair to reward or punish people for actions that are by definition beyond their control. No one can live consistently by any deterministic creed. The Marxist states prove this themselves by their extreme susceptibility to the cult of leadership.

More than that, history refutes the idea that individuals make no difference. In December 1931 a British politician crossing Park Avenue in New York City between 76th and 77th Streets around 10:30 P.M. looked in the wrong direction and was knocked down by an automobile—a moment, he later recalled, of a man aghast, a world aglare: "I do not understand why I was not broken like an eggshell or squashed like a gooseberry." Fourteen months later an American politician, sitting in an open car in Miami, Florida, was fired on by an assassin; the man beside him was hit. Those who believe that individuals make no difference to history might well ponder whether the next two decades would have been the same had Mario Constasino's car killed Winston Churchill in 1931 and Giuseppe Zangara's bullet killed Franklin Roosevelt in 1933. Suppose, in addition, that Adolf Hitler had been killed in the street fighting during the Munich *Putsch* of 1923 and that Lenin had died of typhus during World War I. What would the 20th century be like now?

For better or for worse, individuals do make a difference. "The notion that a people can run itself and its affairs anonymously," wrote the philosopher William James, "is now well known to be the silliest of absurdities. Mankind does nothing save through initiatives on the part of inventors, great or small, and imitation by the rest of us—these are the sole factors in human progress. Individuals of genius show the way, and set the patterns, which common people then adopt and follow."

Leadership, James suggests, means leadership in thought as well as in action. In the long run, leaders in thought may well make the greater difference to the world. But, as Woodrow Wilson once said, "Those only are leaders of men, in the general eye, who lead in action. . . . It is at their hands that new thought gets its translation into the crude language of deeds." Leaders in thought often invent in solitude and obscurity, leaving to later generations the tasks of imitation. Leaders in action—the leaders portrayed in this series—have to be effective in their own time.

And they cannot be effective by themselves. They must act in response to the rhythms of their age. Their genius must be adapted, in a phrase of William James's, "to the receptivities of the moment." Leaders are useless without followers. "There goes the mob," said the French politician hearing a clamor in the streets. "I am their leader. I must follow them." Great leaders turn the inchoate emotions of the mob to purposes of their own. They seize on the opportunities of their time, the hopes, fears, frustrations, crises, potentialities. They succeed when events have prepared the way for them, when the community is awaiting to be aroused, when they can provide the clarifying and organizing ideas. Leadership ignites the circuit between the individual and the mass and thereby alters history.

It may alter history for better or for worse. Leaders have been responsible for the most extravagant follies and most monstrous crimes that have beset suffering humanity. They have also been vital in such gains as humanity has made in individual freedom, religious and racial tolerance, social justice, and respect for human rights.

There is no sure way to tell in advance who is going to lead for good and who for evil. But a glance at the gallery of men and women in *World Leaders—Past and Present* suggests some useful tests.

One test is this: Do leaders lead by force or by persuasion? By command or by consent? Through most of history leadership was exercised by the divine right of authority. The duty of followers was to defer and to obey. "Theirs not to reason why / Theirs but to do and die." On occasion, as with the so-called enlightened despots of the 18th century in Europe, absolutist leadership was animated by humane purposes. More often, absolutism nourished the passion for domination, land, gold, and conquest and resulted in tyranny.

The great revolution of modern times has been the revolution of equality. The idea that all people should be equal in their legal condition has undermined the old structure of authority, hierarchy, and deference. The revolution of equality has had two contrary effects on the nature of leadership. For equality, as Alexis de Tocqueville pointed out in his great study *Democracy in America*, might mean equality in servitude as well as equality in freedom.

"I know of only two methods of establishing equality in the political world," Tocqueville wrote. "Rights must be given to every citizen, or none at all to anyone . . . save one, who is the master of all." There was no middle ground "between the sovereignty of all and the absolute power of one man." In his astonishing prediction of 20th-century totalitarian dictatorship, Tocqueville explained how the revolution of equality could lead to the *"Führerprinzip"* and more terrible absolutism than the world had ever known.

But when rights are given to every citizen and the sovereignty of all is established, the problem of leadership takes a new form, becomes more exacting than ever before. It is easy to issue commands and enforce them by the rope and the stake, the concentration camp and the *gulag.* It is much harder to use argument and achievement to overcome opposition and win consent. The Founding Fathers of the United States understood the difficulty. They believed that history had given them the opportunity to decide, as Alexander Hamilton wrote in the first Federalist Paper, whether men are indeed capable of basing government on "reflection and choice, or whether they are forever destined to depend . . . on accident and force."

Government by reflection and choice called for a new style of leadership and a new quality of followership. It required leaders to be responsive to popular concerns, and it required followers to be active and informed participants in the process. Democracy does not eliminate emotion from politics; sometimes it fosters demagoguery; but it is confident that, as the greatest of democratic leaders put it, you cannot fool all of the people all of the time. It measures leadership by results and retires those who overreach or falter or fail.

It is true that in the long run despots are measured by results too. But they can postpone the day of judgment, sometimes indefinitely, and in the meantime they can do infinite harm. It is also true that democracy is no guarantee of virtue and intelligence in government, for the voice of the people is not necessarily the voice of God. But democracy, by assuring the right of opposition, offers built-in resistance to the evils inherent in absolutism. As the theologian Reinhold Niebuhr summed it up, "Man's capacity for justice makes democracy possible, but man's inclination to injustice makes democracy necessary."

A second test for leadership is the end for which power is sought. When leaders have as their goal the supremacy of a master race or the promotion of totalitarian revolution or the acquisition and exploitation of colonies or the protection of greed and privilege or the preservation of personal power, it is likely that their leadership will do little to advance the cause of humanity. When their goal is the abolition of slavery, the liberation of women, the enlargement of opportunity for the poor and powerless, the extension of equal rights to racial minorities, the defense of the freedoms of expression and opposition, it is likely that their leadership will increase the sum of human liberty and welfare.

Leaders have done great harm to the world. They have also conferred great benefits. You will find both sorts in this series. Even "good" leaders must be regarded with a certain wariness. Leaders are not demigods; they put on their trousers one leg after another just like ordinary mortals. No leader is infallible, and every leader needs to be reminded of this at regular intervals. Irreverence irritates leaders but is their salvation. Unquestioning submission corrupts leaders and demeans followers. Making a cult of a leader is always a mistake. Fortunately hero worship generates its own antidote. "Every hero," said Emerson, "becomes a bore at last."

The signal benefit the great leaders confer is to embolden the rest of us to live according to our own best selves, to be active, insistent, and resolute in affirming our own sense of things. For great leaders attest to the reality of human freedom against the supposed inevitabilities of history. And they attest to the wisdom and power that may lie within the most unlikely of us, which is why Abraham Lincoln remains the supreme example of great leadership. A great leader, said Emerson, exhibits new possibilities to all humanity. "We feed on genius. . . . Great men exist that there may be greater men."

Great leaders, in short, justify themselves by emancipating and empowering their followers. So humanity struggles to master its destiny, remembering with Alexis de Tocqueville: "It is true that around every man a fatal circle is traced beyond which he cannot pass; but within the wide verge of that circle he is powerful and free; as it is with man, so with communities."

1

The Reluctant Avenger

The winding, narrow path through the brambles widened into a small clearing, and Henry of Navarre dismounted from his horse. He could barely hear his soldiers beating drums and shouting as they advanced through the thicket. About three miles back, where the path first branched off the main road, Navarre's keen eye had noticed the fresh tracks of a wild boar.

Only a day before, Henry's quartermaster had purchased grain, casks of wine and cider, fruit, and dried beef, and the supply wagons groaned under the weight of the provisions for his army's march. Still, Henry had spent much of his youth in the mountains and loved hunting, and the thought of a fresh-killed wild pig had stirred his great passion for the sport.

He [Henry of Navarre] was proud of being a Gascon and was not afraid of saying so for he regarded it as a compliment; . . . Although he was a direct descendant of Louis IX he remained all of his life not merely a country gentleman but a genuine man of the people.
—LORD RUSSEL
British historian

Henry inherited the kingdom of Navarre and ruled the province as Henry III. Later, as Henry IV, he became the first Bourbon monarch of France. The Bourbon family name derived from the castle of Bourbon in France.

Prince Henry spent part of his childhood at the home of his maternal grandfather, Henry d'Albret, in the small French village of Coarraze. It was there that Henry developed his interest in boar hunting.

Henry had told his personal guards to dismount, and he had ordered the rest of his army to continue their march under the able command of his trusted aide, the baron of Rosny. The guards had fanned out in a broad line along the road, on both sides of the narrow trail. While the king of Navarre coaxed his horse down the narrow trail through the thicket, hoping to pass the boar, the line of guards began slowly walking through the forest, banging drums and beating the bush with their swords and pikes as they advanced. Slowly, the guards had converged on the trail, flushing the wild boar ahead of them. Henry of Navarre tied his horse at the side of the clearing opposite the point where the trail emerged from the brush.

Navarre left his crossbow, sword, and shield hanging on the saddle, but he pulled a long spear from the scabbard that was belted to the flank of his mount. He checked that his poniard (dagger) had not fallen from its sheath on the belt of his tattered and patched tunic. The tunic was threadbare and dirty and may have been appropriate for a soldier in the field, but it was hardly fit to be worn by the reigning king of Navarre, a man who was next in line to be king of France. However, the year was 1587, and more than 20 years of religious war between France's Catholics and Huguenots had made Henry of Navarre a soldier first and a prince of the royal blood second.

The clashes between Catholics and Huguenots continued the civil strife that had plagued the Valois

The Huguenots were the French Protestants who established a Presbyterian church in France in 1559. They fought religious wars with the French Catholics throughout the second half of the 16th century.

Admiral Gaspard de Coligny, together with Louis I de Condé, commanded the Huguenots in the Wars of Religion against the Catholics. Coligny was the first person killed in the Saint Bartholomew's Day Massacre.

dynasty since its inception. Established as the ruling house of France in 1328, the Valois weathered the Hundred Years' War (1337–1453) with England and subsequently instituted a centralized government to replace the feudal system disrupted by long years of conflict. Though decimated by the war with England, the French nobility resisted the king's authority; in a pattern that would be repeated throughout the Valois dynasty, hostile nobles aligned themselves with factions within the house of Valois in an effort to maintain their influence in the government of France.

Despite such factionalism, France prospered. When Francis I ascended the throne in 1515, his youthful vigor and his penchant for philosophical debate promised an enduring and enlightened reign. But Francis's aspirations proved less profound then the hopes he inspired. Though he indulged even the most radical thinkers, he never intended their thoughts to serve any purpose other than entertainment for the royal court. His chief ambition was territorial expansion. Failing this, he tried unsuccessfully to have himself enthroned as the Holy Roman emperor. Both gambits drew the house of Valois into a power struggle with the house of Habsburg. Their rivalry would be a major contributing factor in the upheaval of the 16th century. Another major factor, arguably the primary factor, was the Protestant Reformation.

The Reformation arose in Germany during the early 16th century. It quickly spread throughout Europe, leaving no country untouched. Where Protestant churches eventually superseded the Roman Catholic church, their success can be attributed to rapid changes in European society. The Roman Catholic church had established its hegemony over feudal Europe. Under the pressure of capitalism, nationalism, and the Renaissance, the feudal system and its values gave way. The authority of the church was further eroded by the corruption that extended from minor church offices to the Vatican, where the Renaissance popes lived in royal splendor.

All Europe has its eyes on you. You are no longer a child. Go and learn under Condé to be a commander.
—JEANNE D'ALBRET
Henry of Navarre's mother, when she presented him with his first suit of armor

Antoine de Bourbon, Henry's father, was the duke of Vendôme and became the king of Navarre through his marriage to Jeanne d'Albret. Antoine rejected his Protestant faith in order to secure relations with the Catholic king of Spain, Phillip II.

The leader of the Reformation was Martin Luther, an Augustinian friar. He vehemently objected to church corruption and implored the church to return to the teachings of Saint Paul, wherein would be found no sanction for the secular privileges enjoyed by the church in modern Europe. Luther also questioned the role of the church as an intercessor between man and God, and branded the ecclesiastical organization a perversion of the true Church of Christ.

The German princes who defended Luther may well have agreed with his theology, but their dispute with the church was political in nature. They endorsed Luther's attack against the ecclesiastical organization because that organization filled the coffers of the Roman Catholic church and financed, in turn, the Holy Roman Empire through which Rome extended its control over Germany. In challenging the spiritual authority of the church, Luther provided Germany with an agenda for liberation from the Holy Roman Empire.

When the Diet of Worms convened in 1521 to investigate the charge of heresy recently leveled against Luther, it was headed by King Charles of Spain, the newly crowned Holy Roman emperor. Having outbid Francis I, Charles gained for the house of Habsburg control of all central and western Europe, except France, England and the Papal States. Though he failed to stem the Reformation in Germany, Charles proved himself in all other cases to be master of Europe and a more than adequate opponent for his contemporaries Henry VIII, king of England, and Francis I, king of France.

The intellectual tolerance practiced by Francis's court provided an opportunity for reformers to exploit the rivalry between the house of Valois and the house of Habsburg. But, though Francis allied himself with the German princes against the Habsburgs, he never envisioned a reformed church of France. In fact, Francis eventually became an opponent of the reform.

Jeanne d'Albret, Henry's mother, was a confirmed Huguenot and refused to renounce her faith when her husband converted to Catholicism. At first, Jeanne took her son to Paris to avoid the "bad influences" of her Catholic husband but was forced by Antoine to return a year later.

Charles IX became king of France at the death of his brother Francis II. Considered weak from the beginning, his rule was dominated by his mother, Catherine de Médicis. Charles died at age 24 of tuberculosis and was succeeded by his younger brother Henry III.

Two events altered Francis's policy: the affair of the placards in 1534 and the publication of John Calvin's *Christianae Religionis Institutio* in 1536. The placards appeared throughout France and attacked the Catholic mass. This act anticipated Calvin's incisive refutation of Saint Thomas Aquinas and the institutions of the Roman Catholic church based on Aquinas's theology. Seeing the church in France threatened in this manner, Francis issued the first of many edicts against the reform.

Francis's son, Henry II, adopted the measures taken by his father. But despite this repression, the French Protestants, or Huguenots, increased in number. Francis's sister, Marguerite of Navarre, offered sanctuary to many threatened Huguenot leaders, and Navarre became an important Huguenot haven. Other nobles also offered their protection. Chief among these were Admiral Gaspard de Coligny and Henry de Bourbon, prince de Condé.

Henry II followed his father's lead in foreign affairs as well. French armies engaged the house of Habsburg in the Low Countries and in Italy. Phillip II, soon after replacing his father, Charles, as king of Spain and Holy Roman emperor, defeated the French at Saint Quentin in 1557. Had Phillip moved swiftly he might have taken Paris. As it was, Francis, duke of Guise, who had distinguished himself in the Italian campaign, headed north in time to relieve Paris.

Guise's successful campaign marked the rise of his political star. He began to play an increasingly influential role in the court of Henry II. A staunch Catholic, he encouraged Henry to sue for peace with Catholic Spain and concentrate all money and arms in a war against the Huguenots and their Swiss and German allies. Though an alliance between Henry and Phillip never occurred, Guise's son Henry would later ally himself with the house of Habsburg in his struggle to keep Henry of Navarre off the throne.

When Francis II succeeded Henry in 1559, he was too young to rule. Guise effectively took control of the government. But, 18 months later, when Francis died and his brother Charles took the throne,

Catherine de Médicis, the mother of the last three kings of the Valois dynasty in France, was the daughter of Lorenzo de Medici, duke of Urbino (a province in Italy). As regent and adviser to her son, King Charles IX, she helped plan the Saint Bartholomew's Day Massacre despite her initial sympathies with the Huguenots.

their mother Catherine de Médicis asserted her right, as guardian, to direct the affairs of state. In a further effort to diminish Guise's power, she invited Huguenot sympathizers into the court. By setting the rival factions against each other, she hoped to neutralize both and thereby keep Charles's throne secure.

During King Charles's reign, Henry of Navarre was confined to the court. His mother Jeanne d'Albret, queen of Navarre, was a confirmed Huguenot. This alone might have made her position at court precarious. But, in addition, her husband, Antoine de Bourbon, hoped to forge an alliance with Phillip II in exchange for compensation for the lands taken from Navarre by Spain in 1512. To secure this alliance, Antoine denounced Protestantism and asked Jeanne to do the same. When she refused, Antoine told her to leave the court and forbade her to take their son Henry with her. Henry's religion became a point of contention. Jeanne had seen to it that he was raised according to the principles of Calvinism upon which the Huguenots based their movement. After forcing Jeanne from court, Antoine placed Henry's instruction in the hands of a conservative Catholic. All means of coercion were exercised in getting Henry to denounce Protestantism, but Henry held fast. How much his religious conviction depended on his devotion to his mother can only be conjectured. Finally, Henry gave in and attended Catholic mass in 1562. It was the first of three nominal conversions to Catholicism.

Antoine was killed at Rouen in 1563 during the first of the Wars of Religion. The Catholic army proved strong enough for Catherine to force the Huguenots to accept the terms of the Treaty of Amboise. A period of peace followed, during which Catherine led the royal court on a tour through France, presenting the king to his subjects. Henry accompanied her entourage, and Jeanne was allowed to join him. With her arrival, the conflict over Henry's religious instruction resumed. In 1567 he and his mother escaped court. When they reached Navarre, the countryside was in trumoil. After Antoine's death, Jeanne had imposed stern measures against Catholics in Navarre. In her absence, Catholics (encouraged by Blaise de Montluc) revolted.

Henry III and Henry, third duke of Guise, would soon be embroiled in the War of the Three Henrys against Henry of Navarre. Henry III eventually changed sides and joined Henry of Navarre's forces, but he was assassinated by a fanatical monk during a siege on Paris.

Now began Henry's military apprenticeship. With her lands in revolt, Jeanne could no longer maintain her neutral status. She headed north and entrusted her son to Henry de Bourbon. His apprenticeship proved brief. In 1569, Bourbon fell at the battle of Jarnac. Here another young warrior, King Charles's brother Henry, carried the day. Following a Catholic victory at Moncontour, Catherine de Médicis arranged a peace between the Huguenots and Catholics. The agreement guaranteed the Huguenots four *places de sûreté* (places of safety) which, with a Huguenot governor and a Huguenot garrison, would offer shelter to Huguenots who were harassed elsewhere. The favorable terms granted the Huguenots expressed Catherine's commitment to maintaining them as viable political opponents to the Catholics who might otherwise turn their demonstrably superior armies against the crown.

According to legend, at the birth of Henry of Navarre the child's grandfather, Henri d'Albret, rubbed the baby's lips with garlic and passed a cup of wine beneath his nose. This ritual has been variously interpreted as a pagan baptism and as a method for warding off the plague.

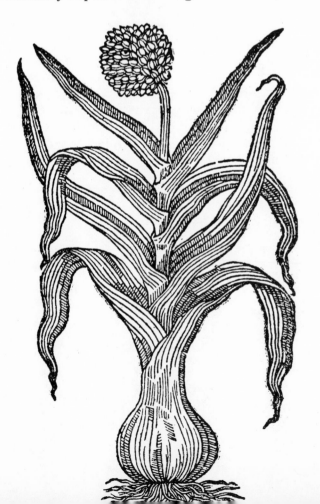

Marguerite of Valois, Henry of Navarre's first wife, was promised to the young prince when he was four years old. The story handed down is that during a visit by Henry of Navarre's parents to the court of Henry II (Marguerite's father), the king was so impressed by the young prince's good looks and manners that he promised his daughter's hand in marriage.

The political division in France was aggravated by a split between moderate and radical Catholics. The moderate faction wished for reconciliation with the Protestants. The radical Catholics were lead by Henry, duke of Guise, whose father, Francis, had been killed by Huguenots. They sought nothing less than the extermination of heretics in France. At first only a tenuously connected group of local Catholic "leagues," the radical Catholics soon organized themselves into an efficient organization, the Catholic League.

The Catholic League declared its purpose in 1584. Impatient with the progress of war against the Huguenots, Henry Guise meant to carry on the war independent of King Henry III. But though the explicit purpose of the League was to keep France Catholic, an ulterior motive was clear. Henry Guise laid claim to the throne, and, with the armies of the Catholic League and the backing of Phillip II of Spain, he planned to make good that claim.

The Huguenots followed the teachings of John Calvin, a French Protestant theologian who rejected the teachings of the Catholic Church. Calvin denied papal authority and embraced the doctrine of predestination — that every person's fate is predetermined.

Henry III became king in 1574 when Charles died of tuberculosis. Though he had showed himself to be an able soldier at Jarnac, Henry was an indecisive and unpopular king. He wavered between his mother's plans and ambitions of his own. His elaborate feasts and games distracted him from the affairs of the realm. He plundered the royal treasury to pay for these expensive entertainments and often had too little money to maintain a standing army.

The formal declaration of the Catholic League coincided with the death of the crown prince, Henry's brother Alençon. Henry's marriage had provided no heirs, so the line of succession passed to Henry of Navarre and the house of Bourbon. However, a Protestant could not be placed on the throne. Henry III sent a delegation to Navarre, carrying a request that Henry return to court and conform to the doctrines of the Roman Catholic church. Henry refused; the way was now open for Henry Guise to place himself or a member of his family in position to succeed Henry III.

The ensuing civil war had yet to yield a victor. By 1587 it was clear that the Huguenots, despite Henry of Navarre's leadership, could not defeat the Catholic League. He grew weary of the struggle and presently wanted to score a decisive victory only so that he and his men could return to their homes as heroes.

At the moment, though, Henry focused his attention on the frightened wild boar. He could hear the commotion his guards were making as they approached. His men had succeeded in flushing the fierce animal ahead of them. Henry readied himself for the onslaught. He pointed his spear toward the place from which he estimated the angry pig would charge, and he wedged the butt of the spear against his foot.

Suddenly, the wild boar leaped from the brush toward the king of Navarre. Henry stood his ground, plunging his spear into the shoulder of the charging boar. For a moment it seemed as though the beast had been stopped, but then the injured animal charged Henry's horse. With the broken shaft of the spear still projecting from its shoulder, the furious boar butted the side of the horse.

Without hesitating, the king of Navarre attacked the boar with his dagger. Finally, the boar fell dead, as the king's guards broke through the brush and into the clearing.

The horse was panicked for the moment but would recover from its wounds. King Henry of Navarre smiled at the scolding his guards gave him for risking his life to save a horse. Henry realized that his loyal troops feared their cause would be lost without their leader.

After the hunt, Henry's officers beckoned him to join them in a game of cards. The normally jovial general declined the invitation as melancholy remembrances crowded out the good mood that a successful hunt normally brought him. His mother and father had been proud when they visited the royal court of King Henry II in Paris. The king had been so impressed by four-year-old Henry of Navarre that he had promised a future wedding between his

> *If I love the table and good cheer, it is because they enliven the spirit.*
> —HENRY OF NAVARRE

daughter Marguerite and the future king of Navarre. Henry's father and mother had married each other for love rather than for political reasons, but nevertheless, they were ambitious, so they sought to arrange a prominent marriage for their son.

Henry's parents regretted that they had very little to leave the young prince of Navarre besides a hatred of the Spanish. In 1512, most of the mountainous kingdom of Navarre had been overrun by Spain. The future wedding between Henry and Princess Marguerite of Valois would provide powerful allies and (Henry's parents hoped) the resources to recapture the areas controlled by Spain.

Henry's sadness for his parents deepened as he recalled how bitterly his parents' lives had ended. They never lived to see their son marry the king's daughter.

Henry's father had died during the siege of Rouen. His mother died in 1572. She had accompanied him to Paris in preparation for his marriage to the princess, but in June she contracted a mysterious illness. Henry had no proof of it, but he suspected that his mother had been poisoned by enemies in the royal court. Although Henry did wed Princess Marguerite, his mother did not live to see the wedding.

The wedding had brought a very brief period of optimism to Henry of Navarre's countrymen. The prospect of a marriage between a Catholic princess and a Protestant prince of the royal blood had filled the French people with hope that the long years of religious warfare might soon end.

The Wars of Religion had devastated France. Marauding armies hired by various French noblemen and foreign troops from Spain, England, and the German and Italian principalities laid waste the countryside. Pillaging soldiers terrorized civilians, and thieves and bandits followed in their wake. When the armies were on the march, they took whatever food and supplies they needed from the nearest peasants. Farmers never knew whether their crops would be stolen or destroyed. Often farmers never bothered to plant, and there was widespread starvation.

Anticipation of the wedding had caused jubilation throughout France. Members of the Protestant and Catholic nobility from all over France gathered in Paris to celebrate the royal wedding that might bring peace, religious tolerance, and prosperity. As Henry considered how that dream had been crushed, a sad expression replaced his smile. Just then a nobleman left the game of cards, approached Henry, and asked him why he was frowning. Henry of Navarre responded that he had remembered the violent events of Saint Bartholemew's Day, shortly after his wedding to Princess Marguerite.

The Protestant nobleman's face contorted with anger. He railed against the hypocrisy of the Catholics, who had broken the divine commandment against murder yet still called the Huguenots heretics. Although the nobleman had no need to describe the events of that day, because Henry had been there, his passionate feelings had loosened his tongue. The nobleman described how King Charles, Henry III's predecessor, had unleashed Henry Guise on the unarmed Huguenot nobles, who were visiting the castle for the wedding of Henry of Navarre and Princess Marguerite. Many had been slaughtered. Only his last-minute conversion saved Henry of Na-

Followers of Calvin destroy the possessions of a Catholic church, including altar paintings and decorative sculpture. Calvinist image breakers sought purity in their religious settings, claiming that images used in religious worship naturally led to idolatry.

varre. The nobleman then recounted how Catholic priests had inspired their parishoners to kill Protestant commoners throughout Paris and the surrounding provinces. Henry had even been held prisoner at the royal court, escaping after four years and renouncing his conversion.

As he spoke, the vehemence of the nobleman's words caught the attention of the other officers at the feast. They drew near and listened to his tirade. He asked if there was anyone present who had not lost a member of his family and declared that the souls of 12,000 innocent Protestants killed in the massacre cry out for revenge against the Catholics.

Henry calmly rebutted his furious aide. He told of the massacre at Nîmes, when Huguenots killed

The Saint Bartholomew's Day Massacre, when French Catholics killed an estimated 12,000 Protestants, began shortly after Henry of Navarre married Marguerite in Paris in 1584. The marriage brought many Huguenots to the capital for the celebration, at which time Catherine de Médicis and Charles IX began the slaughter.

Catholics by throwing them down a well. He reminded his officers that there already had been enough revenge to go around and suggested that it was past time for the killing to stop. After all, both the Protestant martyrs and the Catholic martyrs were French. His heart was heavy with the suffering of his people, and he had no desire to see more bloodshed.

The group that had gathered around the angry nobleman gravely nodded agreement with Henry, and from those men a spontaneous shout went up: "God save King Henry of Navarre!" Henry answered the shout with "God save France!" Then he turned to go to his tent, and the soldiers in his camp fell silent for the rest of the night.

LO SEPTRO DE MILICE.

2

The Battle of Coutras

While Henry of Navarre was asking God to save the kingdom of France, the future of the nation was being discussed elsewhere. Nearly 300 miles from Navarre's bivouac, at the Louvre (the royal palace in Paris), Catherine de Médicis competed against the noise and distraction of the royal court to gain the attention of her son, the king of France.

Amid this frivolity, the queen mother persevered on her mission of state. She wanted to talk about the recent excommunication of Henry of Navarre. (Excommunication, or expulsion from the church, is generally reserved for people who have contradicted church doctrine. An excommunicated person is forbidden to participate in the rites of the church, and it is considered a sin for Catholics to aid an excommunicated person.) Catherine was trying to convince her son that Navarre had made a mockery of Pope Sixtus after the pope had branded Navarre a disbeliever. She implored her son to listen to the inflammatory words that Navarre had written to the pope: "Sixtus V, calling himself Pope, has . . . falsely and maliciously lied, and . . . himself is heretic. . . . The King of Navarre . . . declares him to be Anti-

> *Comrades, we are here for the glory of God and our honor. The road is open before you. On you go in the name of the Lord for whom we are fighting.*
> —HENRY OF NAVARRE
> addressing his troops on the morning of the battle of Coutras

---

Henry IV cutting the Gordian knot, in an allegorical allusion to Alexander the Great. According to an ancient Greek myth, an oracle stated that he who succeeded in untying the Gordian knot would rule Asia. Eventually, Alexander simply cut the knot with his sword and became one of the most powerful leaders of the ancient world.

christ [an opponent of Jesus Christ] . . . and in that quality declares against him a perpetual and irreconcilable war."

However, King Henry believed that the pope had overstepped his bounds by excommunicating a man who was, after all, the king's cousin and brother-in-law and the heir to the throne of France. King Henry resented the pope's interference with the internal affairs of the French nation. He saw the excommunication of Henry of Navarre as an example of this interference and as an attempt by the pope to manipulate the succession to the throne of France. What he did not see was that the excommunication was the work of Henry Guise.

The king's comments made Catherine pause, because she knew that her son's position was threatened from two directions. Naturally, the Protestants

In an attempt to mitigate the growing antagonism between Catholics and Protestants, and thus strengthen the throne of her son Henry III, Catherine de Médicis invited Henry of Navarre to live at the court in the Louvre, the royal palace of France. Distrustful of Catherine's motives, Henry refused but later moved into the palace as king of France.

were hostile, but so, too, were some radical Catholics. Pope Sixtus V had given his blessing to the Catholic League, which owed its primary allegiance to Henry Guise and his brother, the duke of Mayenne. Further, King Phillip II of Spain had more influence with French members of the Catholic League than did the king of France.

However, even if King Henry had wanted to satisfy the League by crushing the Huguenots, this was no simple matter. There were many Protestant strongholds. Huguenot towns, such as La Rochelle and Bordeaux, were fortified, and their populations were heavily armed. Huguenot noblemen had fielded armies to defend the rights of Protestants. Elizabeth I, queen of England and head of the Anglican (Protestant) church of England, had sent weapons and soldiers to help the French Protestants.

The queen mother had to convince King Henry to deal with this dangerous situation. The duke of Mayenne, at the head of a large army of Catholic Leaguers, was due in Paris any day. With King Henry's endorsement, the duke of Mayenne had embarked on a campaign to conquer the Protestant towns loyal to Henry of Navarre. Mayenne's force was much larger than Navarre's, but the duke of Mayenne was inferior to Henry of Navarre as a strategist. Traveling light and fast, Navarre's army had waged guerrilla warfare, attacking stragglers of the duke's huge army and cutting off the duke's sup-

plies. Meanwhile, Mayenne had foolishly wasted his forces by attacking the most strongly fortified Protestant towns.

Catherine saw a means by which King Henry might be able to turn Mayenne's failure to his own advantage. The Catholic League had been weakened by its unsuccessful campaign against Henry of Navarre. Other Catholic League forces, commanded by Henry Guise, were still at France's eastern border, trying to prevent German and Swiss soldiers from linking up with Henry of Navarre's army. Catherine reasoned that Guise would fight to a draw with the

In 1587, Henry of Navarre fought the Catholic League in the Battle of Coutras. The League army (under the leadership of the duke of Joyeuse) had more soldiers and better weapons. Still it proved no match for Henry's superior military strategies.

Pope Sixtus V excommunicated Henry of Navarre following the latter's plea for aid from various European Protestant monarchs to fight the Catholic League. Henry's response, in which he accused the pope of heresy, aroused French national spirit, both Protestant and Catholic.

German and Swiss Protestants; thus, both the Catholic League and Navarre's allies from Germany and Switzerland would suffer losses. With the League weakened and Henry of Navarre simultaneously deprived of aid, Catherine suggested that King Henry's position would be very strong. Both the Huguenots and the Catholic League would profit from an alliance with the king. Henry of Navarre's force was still in good shape, and Catherine reasoned that King Henry should betray Guise and form an alliance with Henry of Navarre.

However, the king realized that Navarre might resist his overtures. Navarre had mocked the pope after the excommunication, and King Henry questioned whether Navarre would be any more accommodating to him. Catherine asked her son to send her as an ambassador to Henry of Navarre. Her strategy was to appeal to Navarre's sense of personal and family allegiance to the king. She would also remind Navarre that he was the heir to the royal throne and try to convince him that it was in his interest to maintain the authority of the throne that he might inherit.

Catherine thought that France would have peace if Navarre would once again renounce his Protestant faith and swear allegiance to the Catholic church. She doubted that Navarre was truly devoted to worshipping as a Protestant, and she reasoned that Navarre would prefer living at court as the crown prince to leading the nomadic existence of an outlaw soldier. Catherine's agents had told her that she could arrange to meet Navarre at the château of Saint-Brice.

King Henry doubted that his mother's plan would work, but he realized that there was nothing to lose by trying. If the negotiations failed, perhaps a Catholic League force led by the duke of Joyeuse would do better against Navarre than had the duke of Mayenne's army. The army commanded by the duke of Joyeuse was well equipped with weapons supplied by Phillip II. At last, the king agreed that Catherine should meet with Henry of Navarre.

Several days later, as Henry of Navarre approached Saint-Brice, 400 of his soldiers watched from the hillside overlooking the château. The precautions were necessary; during the religious wars, treachery and assassination had become commonplace, and the invitation to discuss peace with the queen mother might have been a trap.

Catherine presented the meat of her proposal to Henry of Navarre. She told him that the duke of Joyeuse would abandon his campaign against Navarre's Protestant supporters in the Poitou region if Navarre would end his military operations in the Béarne and Guyenne regions. As part of the deal, Henry would take up residence at her son's court at the Louvre as the legitimate heir to the French throne.

Henry, who was weary of the bloodshed, seriously considered the queen mother's offer. On the surface the proposal seemed straightforward, but he had reasons to be suspicious. He had been held under virtual house arrest the last time he had lived at the royal court, following his wedding. His eventual escape was an example of the cunning he had shown on the battlefield. The day before the planned break-

Catherine was an Italian by birth and [had a] temperment with a passion for power, a ruthless will, a subtle scheming brain, a complete lack of moral feeling, and a callous indifference to the sufferings of those who caused her inconvenience.
—HESKETH PEARSON
author

out, he had spread a rumor that he already had fled, and then he hid for a few hours. Finally, he surprised the king and queen mother by walking in on their discussion of what they would do when they caught him. He put the royal pair at ease by saying he had heard they were searching for him but he wondered why, because although he could easily have escaped, he never would. He built up their confidence by telling them that he wished to continue serving them loyally. Having discouraged their vigilance, Henry fled the castle the very next day, pretending that he was leaving to go hunting.

Henry realized he could always slip away from the Louvre if the court became too restrictive, but other parts of the queen mother's offer disturbed him. The king of Navarre was no Protestant zealot. He believed that there were good and bad people among both the Protestants and the Catholics. In fact, Henry's religious tolerance had helped him to form valuable alliances with a few Catholic noblemen. Henry realized there were many more Catholics than Huguenots in France, and he knew that he would not last long as king of France if his subjects believed that he was hostile to their religion. Catherine's pro-

The Catholic League, which was founded by Henry Guise, sought the suppression of Protestants in France. Although dissolved by King Henry III one year after its formation, the League revived several years later and received the approval of both the pope and the king of Spain.

posed arrangement, however, also would deny the Protestants in Béarne and Guyenne the right to practice their religion. Accepting Catherine's proposal would compromise his belief in freedom of conscience and would constitute a betrayal of his allies. When Henry voiced his objections to Catherine, she replied that he was allowing religion to stand in the way of the peace that she so ardently wanted for their country. Henry, however, recognized the deceit in Catherine's words and would not be swayed.

As Henry of Navarre left the meeting, he did agree to meet with Catherine again the next day. Though he said that he might consider Catherine's proposal to some extent, Henry could not abandon his supporters. With the failure of Catherine's attempt at peace, more bloodshed seemed inevitable.

Numerous small battles did follow the collapse of the peace talks, and Henry's reputation for generosity to his defeated enemies grew alongside his reputation for unparalleled skill as a military leader. However, at the dawn of a crucial battle his forces were dangerously split into two locations.

Early on the morning of October 20, 1587, Henry stood on the ramparts (protective outer walls) of the castle at Coutras and watched a lone horseman approach. The rider was a spy he had dispatched the previous day to locate the army of the duke of Joyeuse. Henry had already sent most of his artillery across the river Dronne. The troops that remained on his side of the river had provided security for an orderly crossing by the artillery forces, and they were now camped in and around the town of Coutras, with only three cannons left for their own protection. If the duke of Joyeuse was nearby, then Navarre's divided forces were in considerable danger.

The agent gained admission to the castle and was escorted up to the ramparts. He reported that the duke of Joyeuse had 2,500 cavalrymen and twice that number of infantrymen and was only a few hours' march away. It appeared that Joyeuse knew Henry's location and was confident of his chances in battle.

Henry Guise participated in the planning of the Saint Bartholomew's Day Massacre and the creation of the Catholic League (originally planned by his uncle, the Cardinal of Lorraine). Guise, who desired the throne of France, was assassinated by order of King Henry III.

The duke of Mayenne succeeded his brother Henry Guise as leader of the Catholic League. He was later defeated by Henry IV (of Navarre) and signed a Peace Treaty at Fontainebleau, the king's country court, in 1596.

Henry turned to face his allies, the baron of Rosny and the duke of Condé. The three men discussed the situation. They would miss the artillery and their troops on the other side of the river, but they could not safely retreat across the Dronne to join them; Joyeuse would fall upon them from the heights while half the army was still fording the river and wipe them out. Henry of Navarre's army was vastly outnumbered, but there was a good chance that his seasoned soldiers could outfight the Catholic League army. Henry announced to his aides that he had studied the terrain, and he would meet the rapidly approaching enemy there in Coutras.

Whatever misgivings Rosny and Condé may have had, they probably kept them to themselves. In all matters of state Henry of Navarre sought the advice of these two loyal aides, but on military matters he acted according to his own judgment. He had a remarkable grasp of military situations and a sharp eye for the best possible strategies. Thus far, his combat decisions in the field had been both successful and ingenious. Condé and Rosny assembled the troops and awaited Henry's orders.

Henry, wearing his characteristic white-plumed helmet, led his troops on a short march from the parade grounds to a nearby field that he had spotted as an ideal defensive position. The king directed his officers to place the three remaining cannons on hills that would dominate the field of battle below. He directed the captains of his cavalry to assemble their mounted soldiers on the high ground. From there, they could sweep down to meet the numerically superior cavalry of Joyeuse as it advanced up the hill. Navarre's horse soldiers were reinforced by foot soldiers, each of whom was armed with a harquebus (a powerful early form of the musket with a heavy barrel that had to be supported by a tripod). The first onslaught of Joyeuse's cavalry would be met by other foot soldiers commanded by the viscount of Turenne.

Queen Elizabeth I of England, the daughter of King Henry VIII of England and Anne Boleyn, reestablished the Protestant faith in England and supported the French Huguenots' fight against the Catholic League.

King Phillip II of Spain sympathized with the Catholics' plight in France. He supported their cause by supplying weapons and armor to the troops of the Catholic League.

Shortly after Henry's army had settled into its positions, the army of the duke of Joyeuse appeared on the horizon and slowly marched toward its adversary. The old and dull armor of Henry's forces was pitiful in comparison to the sturdy, shiny armor of the Catholic League, recently provided by the king of Spain, but Henry remarked that the shiny armor meant that "we shall have the better aim when the fight begins."

As the armies squared off for the battle, Henry knelt to pray. Across the field, the duke of Joyeuse remarked that the prayer was a sign that Henry was frightened. But one of the captains of Joyeuse's army told the duke that the bravest of men pray before entering battle as part of their resolve to conquer or die.

Joyeuse's artillery began firing at Henry's army, and his cavalry began to charge up the hill toward the forces of Navarre. Shooting uphill from behind the Catholic army, Joyeuse's cannons accomplished little more than plowing up the dirt of the hillside. Meanwhile, the bullets from Henry's harquebuses and the cannonballs fired by his three remaining artillery pieces killed and maimed many of the duke's horsemen. The foot soldiers under the viscount of Turenne moved forward to meet Joyeuse's cavalry, but they ran back in fear to Henry's lines, until Henry's cavalry charged forward with the king of Navarre himself at their lead.

Henry led his cavalry on repeated charges against Joyeuse's horsemen and foot soldiers. Henry was always in the thick of the fight, the sight of the white plume on his helmet rallying his outnumbered troops to attack the better-equipped enemy. Finally, the duke of Joyeuse's army turned and ran, hotly pursued by the king of Navarre's ragged Huguenot army. By the end of the battle, Navarre's troops had killed several thousand of the Catholic soldiers, including the duke of Joyeuse, and had themselves suffered only 40 casualties.

When the few survivors of the Catholic force were corraled, one of Henry's captains asked if the remaining Catholics should be put to death. Henry responded that the vanquished soldiers were Frenchmen, not just members of the Catholic League. He permitted his soldiers to take the armor and weapons of those who had died; he took the enemy's cannons, and he took the flags and banners of the survivors. But after the survivors swore an oath to tolerate Protestant worship, Henry returned their horses and personal weapons and allowed them to go in peace.

Henry did not follow his victory at Coutras with a march on Paris. Instead he retreated to Nerac to deliver the captured battle standards to his mistress Corisande. There were additional considerations. Navarre was first in line to inherit the crown. He believed that his Catholic subjects would only fear him if the Huguenot army made him king by overthrowing King Henry. Taking the crown of France at the point of a sword would also set a dangerous precedent: Others might later steal the kingdom

The duke of Joyeuse attends a ball at the court of Henry III in 1581. As he left for the Battle of Coutras, the duke promised Henry that he would return with the heads of Navarre and Condé.

from him by force. Also, it was still possible that King Henry would become Navarre's ally against the Catholic League.

Henry decided that he would permit the leaders of his army to take their troops back to their own homes. He believed that if he thanked the heroes of Coutras and released them from their obligations now, they would gladly serve him in the future. With his army largely disbanded, Henry of Navarre headed for Nerac. He visited many important noblemen on the way. With them he discussed the future of the Huguenot cause and the possible consequences of his victory at Coutras. Undoubtedly,

Henry Guise bore close watching. His victory over the Swiss and German armies the following year (1588) more than compensated for the battle of Coutras, and there was no telling what more would come of his alliance with Phillip II of Spain.

3

The Assassin's Knife

On Friday, May 13, 1588, King Henry III found that he was a virtual prisoner in his own castle. All through the previous night, his mother had tried to make a favorable deal with Henry Guise for the king. Four days earlier, Guise and his army had returned to Paris from two battles. In those battles, the duke of Guise had decisively beaten German and Swiss Protestants who had been on their way to reinforce the army of Henry of Navarre. The victories by Guise ought to have pleased King Henry because the Huguenots were in open rebellion against the king, but Guise's victory meant that both of the factions that posed a threat to the royal throne had won major battles. It had been less than a year since Henry of Navarre had severely beaten the king's ally, the duke of Joyeuse, in the Battle of Coutras.

Now the leader of one of these factions was in Paris. Disenchanted with the indecisive and morally lax King Henry, Parisian Catholics turned out in mass to greet the victorious duke of Guise as their champion. The meaning of this display was not lost on King Henry. He immediately summoned 4,000 mercenary soldiers, stationed outside Paris, to con-

It is by your conduct that you will justify yourself, and I shall judge of your intentions by the effect of your presence in Paris.

—HENRY III
to the duke of Guise,
shortly before Guise
took Paris

Henry of Navarre was a brave soldier and an able military strategist. The white plume upon his hat became both a symbol of glory and a rallying point for his troops during battle.

HENRY III of FRANCE.

London Published as the Act directs, Oct.ʳ 18ᵗʰ 1804, by J.Wilkes.

Henry III, well known for his eccentric behavior at court, lost Paris to Henry Guise in 1588. After escaping from the capital, Henry plotted the assassination of Guise.

tain Guise's army. But the arrival of King Henry's soldiers could not forestall the popular revolt. The people of Paris took to the streets and joined with the duke's soldiers in forcing the mercenaries to lay down their arms. Henry, duke of Guise, had control of Paris. With it he controlled the throne as well.

The celebrating Parisians gave little thought as to why Henry Guise had chosen this moment to take Paris. Few would have imagined that the initiative belonged not to Guise but to Phillip II of Spain. Phillip had engineered the events in Paris in order to distract the French government while the Spanish armada sailed for England.

To keen observers the mutual advantages of this alliance were now clear. Phillip had not failed to notice the conciliatory gestures made toward the Huguenots by Henry III and Charles before him. As long as France pursued the course of reconciliation, Phillip could never be certain that French forces would not defend the princes of Germany, Holland, or even England. In addition, the long rivalry between the house of Habsburg and the house of Valois gave reason for Phillip to assist in installing a new line of kings. Guise, on the other hand, received from Spain the money and arms without which the Catholic League would have remained an unrealized conception.

Now, on the morning of May 13, 1588, a messenger explained the terms that Guise had demanded from the queen mother. The news was not good; the duke was pressing his advantage. He wanted the king to banish his most loyal followers at court, to abolish his 45-man bodyguard unit, and to bar Henry of Navarre from inheriting the throne. He also wanted the king to appoint him lieutenant general of the kingdom and to put members of the Catholic League in charge of all the important government posts.

Upon hearing the duke of Guise's terms, King Henry exited the castle and mounted an already saddled horse. Accompanied by a few guards and servants who had been waiting for him in the stable, King Henry rode out of Paris. As he passed through the gates of the city, King Henry bitterly announced to his attendants that he would never return to the traitorous city unless he was preceded by a conquering and avenging army. Neither conquest nor revenge were in the cards for Henry III, nor was a return to Paris and his royal throne.

At first, Guise was furious when he learned that the king had slipped from his grasp. King Henry's

Ten members of Henry III's loyal bodyguard murder Henry Guise in the king's bedchamber just hours after being ceremoniously presented with their daggers. Following the ambush, Guise dramatically staggered across the room, spilling blood everywhere before collapsing.

escape meant that the duke would lose his opportunity to use the king's power to his advantage. But King Henry was always weak and indecisive. So, over the next few months, the duke got most of what he had demanded anyway. The concessions to the duke included agreeing to the Catholic League's demand that the king wage war against the Protestants.

Henry's formal capitulation to Guise's request was accomplished through the Second Edict of Union. By signing this document, Henry confirmed the Edict of Nemour that Guise had issued in 1585. The three main clauses of the document were as follows: Henry III recognized Charles de Bourbon, younger brother of Antoine de Bourbon, as heir to his throne; Guise was named commander of the royal troops; and Roman Catholicism would be the only religion of France.

The Estates General were convened. Its members took an oath of union, declaring the representative body of France in favor of the Second Edict of Union. The Estates also voted to deny Navarre his rights as First Prince of the Blood, including his claim to the throne. In this way Guise acomplished what he had failed to do three years earlier when, with the aid of the Spanish ambassador to Rome, he had secured the excommunication of Henry of Navarre. Then both Protestants and Catholics had reacted severely to papal interference in French affairs. Now the Estates General, in the name of France, had denounced Henry of Navarre.

The king disliked and feared Guise, but that winter he invited the duke to visit him at his sanctuary at Blois and made a great pretense of affection. In reality, the king intended to arrest the duke. The queen mother, who was 70 years old, had become seriously ill shortly before Christmas, and one afternoon King Henry visited his mother at her sickbed and told her of his plans for the duke. He sensed his mother's death was near, and he needed her advice to hang on to what was left of his royal authority. Reminding his mother that the duke of Guise had conspired against him with King Philip II of Spain, King Henry declared that he would arrest the duke and his brother, Cardinal Guise, and put them both on trial for treason against France. Ultimately, he would execute them both.

Catherine thought this plan was wrongheaded. She reasoned that the duke's popularity would prevent any court in France from convicting him, and if by some chance the duke was convicted, Cath-

Following the assassination of Henry Guise, the king's bodyguards arrested his brother, Cardinal Guise. The following morning the guards murdered the cardinal, burned the bodies of the two brothers, and spread their ashes to avoid the creation of a martyrs' shrine at their burial site.

erine feared that Catholic extremists would break him out of prison and install him on her son's throne. The queen mother urged her son to abandon his plan.

King Henry left his mother's sickroom more uncertain than he was before. The king knew that many people would support him if he acted decisively against Guise. Some Catholics felt that the duke of Guise had overstepped his bounds. A few Catholic nobles recently had sworn allegiance to King Henry, in order to protect the authority of the king's office. Henry of Navarre had even pledged his loyalty to King Henry III and the house of Valois as the rightful head king of France. Henry of Navarre had proclaimed that, upon the king's request, he would take up arms to defend the king from the Catholic League and the duke of Guise.

On the other hand, King Henry also feared the duke's strength and popularity and doubted that he could go on placating the duke. Faced with his mother's disapproval, King Henry came up with an even bolder scheme. He decided to murder the duke of Guise. He would tell no one of his plan, especially not his mother. She would try to talk him out of it, so he knew that he had to act on his own before she died. Only the assassin would be told. Guise would never expect the king to act so boldly while the queen mother was too sick to advise him.

The king summoned Captain Crillon, a mercenary officer in the king's service. The king offered Captain Crillon a large bonus to murder Duke Henry of Guise and his brother, Cardinal Guise. At first, Crillon refused on the grounds that he was a soldier, not a murderer. Then, seeing a way to placate King Henry, Crillon offered to challenge the duke to a duel.

At first, King Henry considered accepting the captain's offer, but then he remembered that the duke of Guise was an excellent swordsman. What if he killed Captain Crillon in the duel? Certainly, the duke and the Catholic Leaguers would guess who had inspired the mercenary soldier to challenge the duke to combat. The king resolved to find less scrupulous candidates for the assassin's job and swore Captain Crillon to secrecy.

King Henry did not have to look far to find assassins. The commanding officer and soldiers of the *Quarante Cinq*, the king's own 45-man guard unit, were more than willing to take on the dirty job. ("*Quarante cinq*" means "45" in French.)

Three days before Christmas, the commander of the *Quarante Cinq* approached the duke of Guise and announced that the king had summoned the duke and his brother to attend the council of state ministers, to be held the next morning, before the king went into religious seclusion for Christmas. To make sure of the duke's attendance, the guardsman added that the king would settle up his debts and would pay the duke for his service as grand master of the household. Because the 45-man guard unit and all the ministers also would be present for the pay ceremony, the council chamber would not be large enough for the group of bodyguards that often accompanied the duke of Guise. The news that his bodyguard would not be permitted to accompany him ought to have made the duke suspicious, but, as King Henry had predicted, the duke never suspected that the king would act while the queen mother was too ill to provide guidance.

At dinner that evening, the duke found a note in his napkin warning that the king planned to kill him the next day. The duke crumpled up the note and threw it on the floor in defiance. When the Guise brothers arrived at the council chambers on the morning of December 23, the king watched them from a room above the entrance. King Henry called for his priest, Chaplain Dourguin, and instructed him to go to the chapel and pray for the success of a deed that would bring peace to the kingdom.

As he entered the building, the duke noticed that the royal archers were waiting at the foot of the stairs that led up to the council room. He must have sensed some danger, because he asked why the archers were present so early in the morning. Captain Larchant, the leader of the archers, replied that they had come to petition the king for more pay and had hoped to ask the duke of Guise to speak for them to the king. Relieved by the simple explanation, the duke promised to do the best he could to get more money for the soldiers.

Soon after the Council of Ministers began its deliberations, Secretary Revol approached the duke of Guise and whispered that the king wished to confer with him in his room. Then an usher led the duke to the king's room In the room, members of the *Quarante Cinq* were waiting for the duke. The duke turned to run, but he was not quick enough. Before he could escape, the royal guards leaped upon him and stabbed him to death.

Immediately after the *Quarante Cinq* killed the duke, they arrested the duke's brother, Cardinal Guise. The next morning, Christmas Eve, the cardinal was taken from his prison and killed by the guards. To prevent their graves from becoming a shrine, the *Quarante Cinq* burned the bodies of the two Guise brothers and scattered their ashes in the Loire River. King Henry also tried to apprehend the third Guise brother, the duke of Mayenne, but Ma-

yenne escaped to Paris, where he became the head of the Catholic League. Later, King Henry arrested many leaders of the Catholic League, but this only made the League more popular and powerful. Disheartened by her son's actions, the queen mother died two weeks after the duke's murder.

His desperate circumstances forced Henry III to make a crucial decision. He chose to ally himself with Henry of Navarre against the Catholic League. It was arguably the soundest decision he ever made. With moderate Catholic nobles still supporting him and an army stationed at Tours, Henry could play a decisive role in the history of France. Doubtless, this prospect appealed to the failed king.

The alliance though was fraught with complications. Chief among these were the differences be-

One year after his accession to the French throne, King Henry IV battled the duke of Mayenne and the Catholic League of Ivry. Outnumbered and without equivalent arms, Henry's cavalry defeated Mayenne and virtually wiped out the Catholic League's army.

tween the Huguenot and Catholic nobles. But Henry of Navarre knew that only peace between the two camps could save the monarchy from the Catholic League and its Habsburg supporters. To this end he met with Henry III at the château of Plessis-les-Tours.

A truce was arranged and a series of victories quickly followed. The duke of Mayenne withdrew to Paris where he would make his defense. The Huguenots and the royal army controlled the surrounding countryside. Henry III and Henry of Navarre set up camp at Meudon and prepared for an assault on Paris, which if successful would place Henry again on the throne. Little could they guess that the campaign would be thrown into chaos and the opportunity to take Paris lost.

4

Revenge for the Christmas Murders

On August 1, 1589, a monk of the Dominican order named Friar Jacques Clément approached King Henry's military headquarters in Saint Cloud, just outside Paris. Jacques Clément was a man with a mission: He believed that God had spoken to him in a vision and had told him that if he killed King Henry III he would be made a saint.

The monk told the sentry outside the king's army headquarters that he had come on important government business and gave him a letter of introduction, which he had already shown to several other sentries on his way through the king's camp. Although he presented what appeared to be a genuine letter of introduction from a loyal supporter of the king, the monk did not expect an immediate audience with the king. After the sentry gave the credentials to a messenger, Clément only lingered in order to learn if and when he would get to see the king. In a departure from normal procedure, Clément was granted an immediate audience with the king.

Henry III bore all the marks of a tyrant: he was a heretic and an enemy of God, turning a deaf ear to protests, relying on the brutality of German mercenaries to impose his will, and putting his subjects to death.
—ROLAND MOUSNIER
author

Henry of Navarre was proclaimed king by the fatally wounded Henry III. His loyalty to Henry III was a key factor in influencing the king to command his courtiers to pledge their allegiance to Henry of Navarre.

After he fled Paris, Henry III made this château in Saint Cloud the home of his court and his military headquarters.

That the king would have agreed to see an unknown monk is not surprising, however. During the eight months since the king killed the Guise brothers, King Henry had sought every possible opportunity to improve his relationship with Catholic priests and monks. King Henry wanted desperately to counteract the hatred that had grown for him among Catholics since he had killed the leaders of the Catholic League.

While members of the king's guard unit looked on, Jacques Clément bowed to the king. The normally routine sign of respect, no doubt, pleased King Henry, because many French Catholic religious leaders had denounced him and declared his rule to be invalid. The pope had excommunicated the king after the Christmas assassinations. Among France's most powerful noblemen, only Protestant Henry of Navarre had rallied to the king's side. The king's noble titles were written on each of the letters

from Catholic leaders that Friar Clément now handed King Henry. King Henry must have thought that the visit from this Dominican monk was a good sign. It seemed to show that the Catholic Leaguers were finally showing him proper respect.

Perhaps King Henry reflected on what Henry of Navarre had said was the best thing to do about the pope's excommunication. More than half a year ago, Navarre had said, "[The best remedy] is to conquer as soon as we can, for if this happens you will get your [papal] absolution absolutely, but if we are beaten we shall be excommunicated, aggravated and reaggravated."

The king might well have reflected that joining forces with Henry of Navarre had been a good idea. Navarre knew how to wage war. Six months ago, the duke of Mayenne was ready to lead an avenging army of Catholic Leaguers against the king, and King Henry feared for his own life. Now, the royal armies of the kings of Navarre and France were camped on the outskirts of Paris. They planned to attack the duke of Mayenne in Paris the very next day. The Catholic League would soon be at their mercy, and this friar was visiting today to express his humble courtesy.

King Henry briefly examined the letters. Friar Clément's letter of introduction said that the friar would convey a secret message for the king's ears only. King Henry asked the friar what his message was. Rather than respond, Jacques Clément looked apprehensively at the members of the *Quarante Cinq* who stood nearby to protect the king. Appreciating the monk's apparent concern about secrecy, the king gestured for the guards to leave the room. Then Clément and the king both leaned forward in order to confer in whispers. Alone with the king, Jacques Clément pulled a knife from his robes and quickly thrust it into the king's belly.

King Henry pulled the knife from the wound with one hand and hit Clément on the head with the other. Then, looking at the bloody knife, the

wounded king screamed to the guards in the next room, "Oh, this wicked monk has killed me — kill him!"

As the king slumped to the floor, Friar Clément turned to face the door. Hoping that his death would bring him martyrdom and sainthood, he waited for the king's guards. The members of the *Quarante Cinq* rushed into the room and killed the monk.

The news of the attack on King Henry quickly traveled the few miles to Henry of Navarre's camp at Meudon. Navarre hurried to Saint Cloud to join the advisors who kept a vigil at the wounded king's bedside. As a result of their conversations that day they concluded that the duke of Mayenne had a hand in the assassination. Clément believed that God had instructed him to kill the king, but Mayenne had probably encouraged him and given him the documents he needed to get past the royal guards. The royal surgeons considered the king's wound to be superficial and thought that he would survive.

King Henry addressed the assembled members of his court and reminded them that Henry of Navarre

On the pretext of conveying a secret message to Henry III, the fanatical Dominican monk Jacques Clément was able to separate the king from his bodyguards and fatally stab him in the stomach. Clément earned his nickname, "Le Capitaine," from his obsessive talk of leading a revolution.

was the rightful heir to his throne and his choice for successor. Then he ordered the Catholic nobles who were loyal to him to swear an oath to support the Protestant Henry of Navarre and to help Navarre punish the Catholic League. The nobles quickly swore the requested oath. When news of the assassination attempt reached Paris, crowds of Parisians took to the streets to cheer. That evening, after Navarre had returned to Meudon, a messenger came to summon him to the king's side again. The king's

Although Henry III's noblemen had pledged their support for Henry of Navarre (shown here), many were in fact opposed to a Protestant king. For this reason and because a large majority of the French people were Catholic, Navarre considered converting when Henry III died.

condition had worsened, and by the morning of August 2, King Henry III had died of his knife wound. When this news reached Paris, the crowds found Jacques Clément's mother and hoisted her to their shoulders, wildly praising her for giving birth to the "saint" who had killed King Henri.

On that note, France ended 260 years of rule by members of the Valois family. Henri III was the 13th and last king of France from the Valois dynasty. Henry of Navarre, the first Bourbon king, was now the rightful monarch of France, but few of his Catholic subjects were ready to accept him as their king. Members of the Catholic League proclaimed an aged cardinal to be the new king. Navarre's rival for the throne was crowned by the League as King Charles X, but his claim to the throne was no more widely recognized than was Navarre's claim.

5

The King Who Bought Paris

Following Henry III's death, Henry of Navarre was faced with a series of difficult questions. Should he go forward with the planned assault on Paris? Should he make plans for a ceremony to crown him king of France? Would Henry III's army stay together and remain loyal to Henry of Navarre? Would the moderate Catholic noblemen keep their promise to Henry III and support Henry of Navarre? To this last question, Navarre had an answer sooner than he might have expected, when the duke of Longueville and a group of other Catholic nobles met with him on the day of the death of Henry III.

One of the Catholic nobles, Marshal d'O, launched into a long explanation of the views of the Catholic nobility. Marshal d'O concluded that many of the Catholic leaders believed that it would be a sin to fight for a Protestant king. They felt they could only support Henry of Navarre if he became a Catholic.

I am a real father to my people and I would prefer not to have Paris rather than have it devastated by the death of so many.
—HENRY OF NAVARRE
on choosing to take Paris
without bloodshed

Soon after the death of Henry III, Henry of Navarre issued a proclamation enforcing religious tolerance between Catholics and Calvinists in France. He also submitted the decision regarding his own religion to a "free council" to be held in six months. His actions convinced the high officials of Henry III's court to recognize him as their king.

Rather than storm Paris, Henry of Navarre attempted to obtain the city's surrender by starving its citizens. He blocked the trade routes by which food was transported from Burgundy and occupied all of the wheat mills in the surrounding countryside.

Henry of Navarre responded angrily to Marshal d'O's speech. He asked the nobles who among them would wish to perfect the joy of the Parisians and destroy an army of thirty thousand men by bringing confusion into it. Then, he reaffirmed his loyalty to the Protestant cause, arguing that a sudden and drastic change of faith indicates only that a man has none at all. He shrewdly asked them if it would be more agreeable to have a king who is without a God. He added that most of the nobles probably would support him once they had thought the matter over, but those of them who did not pause to consider doing so were welcome to seek their wages under other masters. In response to Henry of Navarre's words, one of the Catholic nobles, the baron of Givri, fell to the ground at Henry's feet, declaring his own allegiance and calling cowards those who would not do the same.

When Henry of Navarre returned to his army's camp at Meudon, he undoubtedly conferred with his trusted advisers. Assessing the situation, Henry and his advisers probably agreed that Givri was correct; few of the late king's loyal Catholic nobles would abandon him. They also would have had to concede that some of the nobles who abandoned him would join the Catholic League. Henry must have expected those desertions, but he also knew that he could rely on the unconditional support of a few Catholics. There still remained the possibility of converting to Catholicism to gain the support of the remaining Catholic nobles.

Moving toward that step, Henry wisely agreed to take instruction in the Catholic religion. This was not the same as converting, and it would allow him to bribe a few Catholics with promises of titles and royal pensions once he consolidated his power. His Catholic supporters would be able to answer the misgivings of fellow Catholics by mentioning his instruction in Catholicism. Unfortunately, if he chose this course he risked losing Protestant supporters. No matter what he did he was bound to alienate some Catholics or Protestants. Too much blood had been spilled in the religious civil wars to allow either side to accept compromise easily.

Few of Henry of Navarre's Protestant supporters would have converted with their leader, and it is doubtful that Henry would have expected them to do so. Still, Henry probably felt that those supporters who would decline to convert if he converted would still be able to set an example for other Protestants by maintaining their loyalty to Henry. Henry did not immediately take any further steps toward conversion, but the germ of a strategy had been planted.

Turning to more immediate concerns, Henry had to call off the attack on Paris. Matters would have been different if Friar Clément had waited just a few days to kill the king. Then, Henry of Navarre would have been conferring with his advisers at the Louvre in Paris, not at a camp in Meudon. Because he could not invade Paris until he had announced his reli-

From whom can you expect such a change of faith except from a man who has none at all?
—HENRY OF NAVARRE
to Marshall d'O

gious position and determined the loyalties of the moderate Catholic nobles, Henry had no choice but to march his army northwest to Normandy. There he would be able to control the ports on the English Channel, so he could still receive the weapons that England's Queen Elizabeth had offered.

Over the next two years, Henry of Navarre led his army (at first composed mostly of Huguenots and a few Catholics) in a campaign to keep the English Channel ports open. The aid from England that came through those ports was his army's lifeline.

On several occasions, the large, well-equipped army of the duke of Mayenne caught up with Henry

The Louvre, the French royal palace, is on the right bank of the river Seine in Paris. In order for Henry to be recognized as the legitimate king of France, it was necessary that he oust the duke of Mayenne from Paris and establish his own royal court at the Louvre.

of Navarre. Each time, Henry displayed the same courage that he had shown in the Battle of Coutras. He led his men to victories that would have been defeats if his soldiers had not rallied to the sight of his helmet's white plume waving to and fro in the thick of battle. Henry of Navarre often spared the lives of his defeated French countrymen, but he showed no mercy toward the foreign mercenaries who served the duke of Mayenne. When enemy forces wished to surrender, Henry's reputation for fairness and compassion made written guarantees of safety unnecessary for the defeated troops. Each time that Henry of Navarre occupied a town or won a battle, more and more moderate Catholics joined his side. Gradually, his Protestant army was transformed into an army of French national unity.

Twice, Henry of Navarre's troops were in a position to take Paris in battle, but Henry refused to seize the city by force. The first time Henry could have captured Paris, he had defeated a larger force of the duke of Mayenne. The duke's army had destroyed a bridge behind itself as it retreated, leaving them trapped across a river and unable to defend the capital. Instead of attacking Paris, Henry kept his army outside the city. In the meantime, the Catholic League reinforced Paris, making a military conquest too costly for Navarre.

The second time Henry was in a position to conquer Paris was during the summer of 1590. On that occasion, his army surrounded and blockaded the city. Henry had decided to starve Paris into submission, but he was horrified when he heard stories that people in Paris had been reduced to eating rats and human corpses as a result of the siege. He relented, giving the women and children permission to safely leave the city. When one of his officers learned that food was being smuggled into Paris and asked Henry how he wanted that stopped, Henry responded that the hungry Parisians were his subjects, too, and he could not stand to see them suffer. He told his soldiers to look the other way when they discovered that somebody was smuggling food into the city. He felt that his country had been hurt enough by the evil religious warfare. The approach of a hostile army finally forced Henry to abandon the siege and chase the enemy.

Henry of Navarre's heart was heavy over the hardships caused by a generation of civil war when he reached an important decision in 1593. As always, he consulted his friend and trusted adviser, the baron of Rosny. Henry had concluded that the most important Catholic nobles would turn against him and join the Catholic League if he remained a Protestant much longer, and Rosny agreed with that conclusion. But the king also feared that the majority of Protestants would turn against him and

What you can see is not everything. You have forgotten that I have God on my side.
—HENRY OF NAVARRE
to one of Mayenne's officers

Henry of Navarre is reported by some biographers to have said, "Paris is worth a Mass," prior to the dramatic ceremony at Saint Denis in which he converted to Catholicism.

choose a new leader if he became a Catholic. Rosny, who was a devout Protestant, disagreed with the second conclusion, claiming that the king's fears were ungrounded. Rosny told the king that he believed very few Protestants would turn against him if he allowed them to worship freely.

Henry was encouraged by his adviser's optimism, but it puzzled him that a staunch Protestant might be so open-minded about the possibility of conversion to Catholicism. Would not other devout Protestants view the conversion as heresy or at least betrayal? Rosny reassured the monarch, telling him that both religions shared the same beliefs. Rosny said that the religions only differed in *how* to honor God. Although Rosny personally believed that the Catholic religion had chosen the wrong path to worshiping God, he believed that choosing one form of Christianity did not oblige worshipers to persecute those who had made the opposite choice. He went

After Pope Clement VIII recognized him as the "Christian King of France," Henry of Navarre was crowned Henry IV by the bishop of Chartres on February 27, 1594.

so far as to say that God had probably given Henry the idea of converting so that Henry could set an example to the rest of Europe of how Christians of different faiths could live together in peace. So far, religious rivalries had caused too much tragedy, disorder and disaster. Rosny said that Navarre could bring Huguenots and Catholics together through faith in God's charity. Or, at least, he could treat both sides so fairly that they would be able to live together in peace and prosperity.

The prospect of peace and prosperity was so attractive to Henry of Navarre that he resolved immediately to search his heart for the Catholic within him.

The religious conscience of Henry of Navarre had long been a point of contention for French theologians seeking to influence politics. Any time Henry changed his mind, he needed strong arguments in order to debate the theologians who opposed his choice. A few days after the discussion with the baron of Rosny, a Protestant minister asked Henry of Navarre how he could even consider converting to Catholicism. Henry asked the theologian if he thought that he would go to hell for converting to Catholicism. Wary of condemning Henry to hell, the minister tactfully responded that if the king personally believed in God, it would not matter whether he had erred by listening to a Catholic priest. Henry pointed out that the minister had conceded that he might still go to heaven even though he became a Catholic. Realizing that he had been trapped by a skillful debater, the minister reluctantly admitted that Catholics can go to heaven because Catholics also honor God. The king rendered his conclusion more emphatically, saying that prudence required that he be Catholic; that way he is saved according to both Catholics and the Protestant minister, whereas being Protestant he would only be saved according to the minister but not according to Catholics!

Henry also talked to Catholic theologians, and he went to the town of Saint Denis to receive more lessons in Catholicism. Some Catholic priests from Paris even risked the anger of the Spanish soldiers, sent by the Habsburgs to take charge of the city, in order to preach to King Henry. Henry pointed out to the Catholic curé (priest) of Saint Eustacia that the Catholic League and their Spanish supporters did not want him to become a Catholic because they feared that they would lose their power if his Catholic subjects felt free to follow him. Henry asked the curé why he risked the anger of the Catholic League. The curé answered that even if the pope himself told him not to instruct Henry in the Catholic faith, the teachings of the church and his conscience demanded that he help a heretic who wished to convert. He said he was obliged to respond to the king's wish to convert.

Although he had been crowned Henry IV, it was still necessary for the king to regain control of Paris. Henry's trusted adviser, Baron Rosny, felt that it was impossible to take the city peacefully, but Henry preferred to make a nonviolent entry into the capital.

Thus, on Sunday, July 25, 1593, Henry of Navarre approached the Catholic church at Saint Denis. As the royal procession made its way down the flower-strewn streets, French, Scottish, and Swiss guards cleared a path for the king through the crowd. As he approached the door of the church, the crowd roared *"Vive le roi!"* (Long live the king!)

At the church door, the crowd hushed so the archbishop of Bourges could ask Henry of Navarre who he was and the purpose of his visit. Henry replied

that he was a humble king who sought to be received into the Apostolic and Roman Catholic Church. The archbishop then asked if that was Henry of Navarre's true intent. The king responded that it was and fell to his knees to deliver a prayer declaring his faith.

Then Henry entered the church, prayed briefly at the altar, attended the mass, and confessed his sins to the archbishop. When the solemn ceremonies ended, Henry of Navarre emerged from the church.

One week after Henry's coronation, the duke of Mayenne fled Paris, leaving the Catholic League and its 4,000 Spanish soldiers without a leader. Henry then bribed the city's appointed governor, the count of Brissac, to allow his troops to enter the city without bloodshed.

The next morning, the ceremony in Saint Denis raised urgent conversations in Paris. The duke of Feria (the Spanish general whose troops controlled the city) and the duke of Mayenne knew that Navarre had been cheered wildly by the Parisians even though they had issued an edict against going to Saint Denis to witness the "false conversion."

The pope's legate could not excuse the disobedience of the archbishop of Bourges. By receiving Henry of Navarre into the Catholic church, the archbishop had gone against the pope's wishes. The duke of Mayenne's greatest worry was a rumor that Henry of Navarre planned to have himself officially crowned king, now that he had demonstrated strong support among both Catholics and Protestants.

During the next three months Henry of Navarre called a truce in his military campaigns, and, without any military pressure, many Catholic towns switched sides to join Henry's campaign against the Spanish-supported Catholic League. Another relatively quick outcome of the conversion was the coronation of Henry of Navarre as King Henry IV. A new crown had to be made for the occasion because the Catholic League had melted down the old one to make gold coins to finance their operations. The ceremony took place at Chartres, on February 27, 1594, about a half year after the conversion. (Reims, the traditional site for coronations of French monarchs, was still under the control of the Catholic League.) Finally, Henry of Navarre was king of France.

Amid the celebration of the coronation, both King Henry and the baron of Rosny agonized about what should be done next to consolidate Henry's power. So far, their strategies had worked, and most of France recognized Henry of Navarre as king. However, Paris itself (the most important city of France) was still occupied by Spanish soldiers and supporters of the Catholic League. True, Parisians had rejoiced when Henry became a Catholic, but that only made the present situation more perplexing. Henry of Navarre could hardly call himself King Henry IV if he could not even safely visit the capital of his country.

Baron Rosny knew that Henry had enough soldiers to conquer the city, but he also knew that King Henry did not want to enter his capital that way. Henry was reluctant to spill more blood now that an end to the religious civil wars seemed to be almost at hand. The baron wondered how his king could take Paris without violence. Eventually, they hit upon a clever strategy to capture the city.

At the time that the count of Brissac had been apointed governor of Paris by the duke of Mayenne, he had relished the thought of the tax money he would get from the Parisians. Now the events following King Henry's coronation kept Brissac too busy to worry about filling his pockets. Only a week

A king without a kingdom, a husband without a wife, a general without money.
—HENRY OF NAVARRE
satirizing himself

after the coronation, the duke of Mayenne and his closest supporters had left Paris for a refuge in the town of Aisne. That took care of part of the dilemma that had so perplexed the baron of Rosny; with the duke of Mayenne out of the picture, Henry of Navarre's assault on Paris could be considerably less violent. However, Mayenne's departure also posed an enormous problem for the count of Brissac.

With the duke of Mayenne gone, the count had only a few diehard Catholic Leaguers and the duke of Feria's 4,000 Spanish soldiers to maintain his control of Paris. The walls of Paris were strong, but Henry of Navarre had many more troops than the duke of Feria and was a superior general. The people of Paris resented having Spanish troops quartered among them, and most of them openly cheered when Henry was crowned at Chartres; there was a strong possibility that they would side with Henry's invasion force.

The answer to Brissac's dilemma was an agreement with the king to "sell" him Paris. For turning over the keys to the gates of the city, Brissac would receive a royal title. Brissac also would receive a royal pension (a regular payment from the king). For Brissac's cooperation, the king also offered him the governorship of two towns and a substantial cash payment.

The duke of Feria trusted the count, and the count thought it would be simple to deceive him. However, fooling the duke of Feria proved to be difficult. On Monday, March 21 (the day before the planned betrayal of the Spanish garrison), the duke of Feria became suspicious. The duke insisted that Spanish soldiers accompany the count of Brissac when the count made his night's inspection of the gates of Paris. The history of France might have been very different if King Henry's soldiers had arrived early. The Spanish soldiers probably would have carried out their secret orders to kill the count if any enemies approached the gate, but Henry's troops were not at the gate at the appointed hour and the duke of Feria's suspicions were allayed.

After his rounds with the soldiers, the count of Brissac and several trusted companions returned at

about three o'clock Tuesday morning to a gate of Paris called Porte Neuve. All the Spanish soldiers had returned to their quarters to sleep. Count Brissac and his accomplices opened the gate and lowered the drawbridge. The count and one other man walked out onto the drawbridge and peered into the rainy pre dawn for signs of the king's army. All was quiet.

After about an hour the vanguard of King Henry's army emerged. The rain had delayed the army's advance, but soon Henry of Navarre's disciplined and

Late at night, as the 4,000 Spanish soldiers occupying Paris slept, Henry and his troops were quietly let into the city via the gate at the Porte Neuve. Henry's men took control of the capital quickly and peacefully.

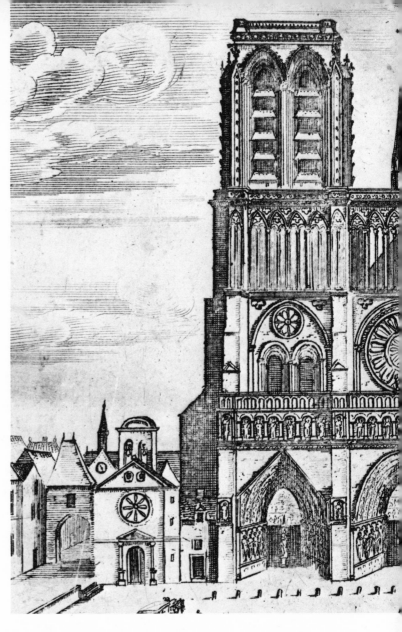

loyal soldiers were marching into Paris. Quietly, the soldiers took control of the city's bridges, defensive positions, and public squares. Henry's troops pulled the cannons off the city's walls and turned them around to point down the main streets. After a few hours, Henry himself, wearing his armor and accompanied by 400 of his cavalrymen, entered Paris.

The Spanish army awoke to the sound of Parisians celebrating the peaceful invasion by King Henry of Navarre. Soon after Henry entered the city, he went to Notre Dame cathedral to hear a Catholic

After his entry into Paris, Henry IV went directly to Notre Dame to hear Catholic mass and to give thanks to God. The cathedral's bells rang out, alerting the supporters of the Catholic League of Henry's success.

mass. Then he went to the Louvre. The mood of Paris was jubilant. The bells of the great churches were ringing, and the citizenry took to the streets to shout, "*Vive le roi!*"

Navarre sent a message to the duke of Feria, whose soldiers were still in their quarters. The message said that the lives of the Spanish troops would be spared if they left Paris immediately. Within two hours of the delivery of the message, King Henry watched the Spanish garrison march out the Saint Denis gate of Paris.

6

The Reign of Henry IV

When King Henry took Paris in 1594, it was impossible to know whether the warfare had truly ended. The religious hatred of the civil wars still burned in the hearts of both Catholics and Protestants. Many of Henry's Protestant supporters wanted him to punish the members of the Catholic League, but the new king offered generous pardons to almost all his former enemies. Because Henry had become a Catholic, many Catholic leaders hoped that he would turn against his former Protestant supporters. Instead, King Henry issued the Edict of Nantes in 1598. The edict granted Protestants the right to hold office and to worship publicly in certain cities (they were barred from worshiping in Paris and in cities where cathedrals were located) and opened a new era of religious tolerance in France. Henry also built bridges of friendship to the leaders of the forces that had opposed him. By offering royal pensions, titles, and gifts, Henry bribed his former enemies to become his loyal supporters.

I am a shepherd King, who will not shed the blood of his sheep, but seek to bring them together with kindness.
—HENRY OF NAVARRE
upon issuing the Edict
of Nantes

In 1600, following the annulment of his first marriage, Henry IV married the Tuscan princess Marie de Médicis. This marriage was of great economic advantage for France because the country owed the bride's uncle, Grand Duke Ferdinand de Médicis, enormous sums of money. The Médicis had largely paid for Henry's campaigns against the Spanish.

Entrée
d'Henri IV
a Paris

HENRI IV
Roy de France

Henri IV
signe l'édit
de Nantes

This triptych depicts the entry of Henry IV into Paris (left panel) and the signing of the Edict of Nantes (right panel). The Edict was later revoked by Cardinal Richelieu, chief minister to Henry IV's son Louis XIII, who sought an absolute centralization of royal power.

Meanwhile, the new king still had some powerful enemies, and a few nobles hatched plots to kill or overthrow him, but King Henry managed to stay ahead of the intrigue. In 1594, a Jesuit priest named Jean Châtel had attempted to kill the king. The plot was foiled, however, and Henry used the plot as an excuse to expel the Jesuits (at that time a very powerful order of Catholic monks) from France.

There were major factions Henry could neither convince nor bribe to end their opposition. The most tenacious of these factions were from Brittany, a region in northeast France. The people of Brittany (called Bretons) were backed by King Phillip II of Spain, so their opposition was a serious matter. In 1595, Henry declared war on Spain.

Over the next three years, Spain captured several cities, but Henry was able to recapture most of them. The war ended in 1598 with the Treaty of Vervins. Under this treaty, Spain was allowed to maintain control of the city of Cambrai but was required to withdraw all other forces and to stop supporting the Bretons. Breton allegiance was finally secured through the arranged marriage of one of Henry's illegitimate sons to the daughter of a prominent Breton nobleman.

Throughout the rest of Henry IV's reign there were minor skirmishes. Henry also added to the territory of France by annexing the possessions of some independent noblemen. However, Henry had accomplished something that his predecessors had been unable to do: He brought an end to the terrible religious civil wars that had lasted more than 40 years and he brought a new sense of political unity and national identity to France.

As king, Henry IV set about reviving France's economy, which was in shambles after the 36 years of religious wars. He encouraged the growth of national industries and in particular reestablished the silk industry.

Henry IV bows to his mistress Gabrielle d'Estrées, famed for her "lovely double-chin." The love affair was never kept a secret from the French people, and the two were often seen together in public with Gabrielle receiving royal honors.

After decades of war France was in a shambles: The government was nearly bankrupt; agriculture and industry were both in disarray; famine was widespread. With the wars at an end, Henry IV began the formidable task of rebuilding France.

The reign of Henry IV is remembered as a period of great economic growth. Led by Henry and his finance minister, the baron of Rosny, France established itself as a major economic force in Europe. Henry's government encouraged the growth of new industries (notably silk) by granting subsidies to businesses. Rosny instituted a series of financial reforms that stabilized the national treasury. Under Henry IV, the French government also began a policy of selling certain government offices. Although in later reigns this practice was the source of much corruption, it provided a large source of revenues for the national treasury.

Henry's policy of challenging foreign industries by building industry at home and encouraging the export of French goods was an early form of *mercantilism*. Mercantilism was an economic theory that held that the basis of a nation's wealth was in the accumulation of gold through international trade. Mercantilism came to dominate international affairs in the nearly 200 years following Henry's reign and was a driving force behind the creation of the European empires of the 18th and 19th centuries. Henry IV's achievements in stablizing the politics and economy of France made him one of the most honored and respected monarchs in European history.

After the death of his first mistress, Gabrielle, Henry IV soon became romantically involved with Henrietta de Balzac d'Entragues, the 18-year-old daughter of the governor of Orleans. Henry refused to honor his marriage contract with Henrietta and instead married Marie de Medicis.

Henry IV and his wife Marie de Médicis are depicted in these two ivory carvings. Prior to his departure for military campaigns against the Catholic Habsburgs, Henry crowned his wife and gave the queen the power to rule France in his absence.

Most of the ordinary citizens of Paris idolized the new king. King Henry won favor in largely Catholic Paris by faithfully celebrating all the Catholic holidays and by worshiping with his subjects at each of the major Catholic churches of Paris.

Initially, many French Catholics believed a rumor that Henry of Navarre had once said cynically, "Paris is well worth a mass," meaning that a sham conversion to Catholicism was a small price to pay for consolidating his power. However, the rumor faded, and most French Catholics came to accept the sincerity of Henry's conversion. Despite the conversion, his Protestant subjects also trusted him. The Protestants remembered his past military protection and valued the guarantees of religious freedom granted by the Edict of Nantes.

After decades of civil war, most of the people of France were happy to have a king who had stood up to King Phillip II of Spain instead of fighting other French leaders. After years of internal warfare and famine, here was a king who said, "Should God let me live longer I will see that no peasant in my realm lacks the means to have a chicken in his pot," and worked to strengthen the French economy so that this might come to pass.

Although Henry's leadership was a source of admiration, his personal life was a virtually endless source of gossip and scandal. He had had many affairs and had several illegitimate children. In 1599, the pope agreed to annul Henry's first marriage to Marguerite of Valois so that the king could marry his mistress, Gabrielle d'Estreé, who had al-

Marie de Médicis was the daughter of Francesco de Medici, grand duke of Tuscany. Francesco was devoted to alchemy, an interest Marie made her own at an early age and that she continued to pursue as queen of France.

ready borne him a son. Shortly before the wedding, Gabrielle died while giving birth to another child. Later in 1599, Henry married Marie de Médicis. In 1601, Marie gave birth to a son who would eventually become King Louis XIII.

Thus, in May 1610, Henry of Navarre should have felt confident, even though he was planning a risky war against the Austrian house of Habsburg, which ruled the remnants of the Holy Roman Empire, a loose confederaton of states owing allegiance to the pope. In this war, Henry's powerful royal army of 40,000 soldiers would help Protestant German princes drive forces of the Catholic Hapsburgs from a province called Cleves-Julich. Judging from the condition of the French army, the campaign probably would be successful. In preparation for his departure for the military campaign, the king had

Marie de Médicis became regent for her son Louis XIII at the death of her husband, Henry IV.

Louis XIII succeeded his father as king of France at the latter's death in 1610. Louis was only nine years old at the time.

formally crowned Marie queen and appointed her to rule in his absence. (His son, Louis, was only eight years old at the time.)

It was true that many individuals still harbored grudges from the religious civil wars. However, by 1610, Henry IV's authority was no longer challenged by any powerful leaders in France. Henry of Navarre trusted the people of France and often was careless about security, despite the fact that during his life there were 20 attempts to assassinate him. The king's bodyguards worried greatly about his habit of occasionally going out among the people with only a few other nobles as escort. But Henry believed that his people loved him, and he usually did not fear an attack. This made it difficult to protect him from a determined assassin. The king was confident no harm would befall him on his outings, but he should have feared one man, a penniless ex-schoolmaster named François Ravaillac.

Shortly after Easter in 1610, François Ravaillac was walking on the road from Paris to his birthplace at Angoulême, mumbling to himself as he plodded down the road. As he walked, Ravaillac's mind was immersed in a jumble of confused and angry thoughts. He had not understood why the Jesuits had failed to believe in his fervid love of God and had kept him from joining their religious order. The Jesuits had said that Ravaillac was unacceptable for their order because he had been a member of another order, the Feuillants. Ravaillac would have stayed in the Feuillant order, but they had thrown him out because he believed that the Lord had appeared to him in visions. The Feuillants thought that Ravaillac was possessed by evil spirits. Ravaillac believed that the visions of God were real.

Ravaillac had journeyed to Paris believing that God had sent him there to kill the king. He was plagued by doubts, fearing that it was actually Satan who had instructed him to kill the king. He had broken the point off his stolen knife because he feared God did not really want him to kill the king, and finally he had decided to go back home and confess his thoughts to his village priest.

It is an offense to God to give credit to astrology, and—having God as my guard—I fear no man.
—HENRY OF NAVARRE on hearing prophecy that he might be assassinated

Ravaillac had also made a trip to Paris the previous Christmas. On that occasion, Ravaillac believed that God had told him to convey a message to the king. He had written God's instructions on a scroll — the message instructed the king to force the Protestant Huguenots to return to the Catholic religion — and had attempted to give the scroll to King Henry as he rode by in his royal coach. The guards had pushed him away from the king, and the message went undelivered. After he failed to give his scroll to the king, Ravaillac saw the first vision in which God told him to kill the king.

Ravaillac had been confused that Christmas by his visions, so he left Paris. Now, leaving Paris for

RACE PARFAITE, DEDIÉ
ARE MAIN, A GARDÉ NO:
RA LA SEIGNEVRIE DV
TERRE ET MER A
ERRANT
DHEVR YRA EN
ARMEE AY:
INCORA

This allegorical engraving shows Henry (upper left) with his wife and child (upper right). The French coat of arms, the fleur-de-lis, can be seen on Henry's clothing as well as on that of the queen.

the second time, Ravaillac was still uncertain about his vision. Rumors were circulating that King Henry planned to kill all of France's Catholics to avenge the Saint Bartholomew's Day massacre of Protestants and that Henry planned to fight a war against the pope, God's representative on earth. As he walked into the town of Étampes, Ravaillac's indecision mounted. The king's attack on the pope would be an attack on God. Should not Ravaillac kill a man to defend God? Ravaillac frantically asked God to send him a sign.

Just then Ravaillac passed a church, where an engraving of Christ's agony on the cross was displayed. The sight of the blood pouring from Christ's

Henry IV bids his family farewell as he departs for military campaigns in Germany. Henry had devised a "Great Design" to free European countries from the menace of Habsburg rule.

wounds was the sign that Ravaillac sought. Ravaillac fell to his knees and pulled the knife from his cloak. He found a stone by the roadside and slowly began to grind a new point on the broken blade. When he had repointed his weapon, Ravaillac stood up and retraced his steps to Paris. There, Ravaillac stalked the king for several days, but could not get close enough to carry out his crazed mission.

On Friday morning, May 14, 1610, King Henry was to leave Paris for his military campaign against the Habsburgs and was growing restless at the Louvre. He decided to call on Baron Rosny to discuss the preparations for the war. Baron Rosny, whose duties included supervising the forging of cannons, was at the arsenal in the fortress called the Bastille.

Normally King Henry's coach would be accompanied by guards, but on this particular morning the king rejected his escort. He had other jobs for the guards. The queen planned to celebrate her recent coronation later that day by making a ceremonial entrance to the Louvre castle, and the king wanted the guards to make certain that everything was prepared for the event. So with only a few noblemen in the horse-drawn coach and a few servants alongside, Henry set out across Paris to the Bastille.

King Henry was wearing his breastplate, but because of the warm spring weather he wore that piece of armor loosely and untied. The leather curtains of the coach were also open because of the weather.

Ravaillac, who was still stalking the king, was waiting at the Louvre when the coach departed. He followed the slowly moving coach on foot.

Queen Marie de Médicis placed great faith in the predictions of her court astrologers. Henry IV's anxieties and fears concerning his plan against the Habsburg monarchy were reinforced by these astrologers. On a regular basis they predicted his death and ruin.

On May 14, 1610, Henry IV was assassinated by the fanatic, perhaps schizophrenic, François Ravaillac. Ravaillac believed at various times that he received messages from both God and Satan and later confessed his belief that Henry was plotting a war to overthrow the pope.

The coach had to travel down a crowded street called the *rue du Ferronnierie*. An earlier French king had decreed that the shops and market stalls that clogged that street be torn down to relieve the crowding, but that order had been ignored. King Henry's coach was caught in a traffic jam. The king's coachmen went ahead of the vehicle to clear the path. While the coach was stopped, Ravaillac leaped

I am wounded. It is nothing.
—HENRY OF NAVARRE
shortly before his death

from the crowd onto a wheel of the coach. Before anybody could stop him, Ravaillac reached into the coach with his knife, and twice plunged the knife through an opening in the breastplate, into the king's chest.

King Henry died before his coach could bring him back to the Louvre. The duke of Epernon, who was riding in the coach with the king, prevented anybody from killing Ravaillac at the scene of the murder. Because the nobles of King Henry's court could not believe that a commoner would act alone to kill the king, Ravaillac was tortured and questioned several times during the next few days in the hope that he would reveal who had inspired him to assassinate the king. Ravaillac only confessed that he believed his instructions came directly from either God or Satan. No nobleman or foreign prince was ever implicated in a conspiracy to kill Henry of Navarre. Finally, Ravaillac, while still conscious, was publicly drawn and quartered. The crowd that witnessed the execution burned the pieces of Ravaillac's body.

Henry IV has been remembered since his death as "Henry the Great." His charm, wit, and love for the common man have become legendary.

This death mask of Henry IV was retrieved in 1793 when the monarch's tomb at Saint Denis was desecrated. The ruling house of Bourbon, established by Henry IV, lasted until the French Revolution in 1789.

The dynasty founded by Henry of Navarre lasted until the French Revolution, 179 years after his assassination. The house of Bourbon also briefly ruled England under Charles II.

Although the French Revolution of 1789 sought to discredit the previous centuries of monarchy, it failed to destroy affection for Henry of Navarre. After the revolution, Napoleon Bonaparte removed the statues of French kings from the Tuileries palace in Paris — all the statues except that of Henry of Navarre. In France, many people still call him "Henry the Great."

Further Reading

Mahone, Irene. *Royal Cousin*. New York: Doubleday, 1970.

Mousnier, Roland. *The Assassination of Henry IV*. London: Faber and Faber, 1973.

Pearson, Hesketh. *Henry of Navarre: The King Who Dared*. Westport, CT: Greenwood, 1976.

Roelker, Nancy L. *Queen of Navarre, Jeanne D'Albret*. Cambridge, MA: Harvard University Press, 1968.

Russell, Lord of Liverpool. *Henry of Navarre*. New York: Praeger, 1969.

Seward, Desmond. *First Bourbon: Henry IV, King of France & Navarre*. Boston: Gambit, 1971.

Chronology

Dec. 13, 1553	Henry of Navarre is born at the Château de Pau
Feb. 1557	His marriage is arranged to Marguerite of Valois, daughter of King Henry II
1562	Wars of religion between the Huguenots and Catholics of France begin
1569	Henry joins the Huguenot army
Aug. 18, 1572	Marries Marguerite of Valois and becomes King of Navarre
Aug. 24, 1572	St. Bartholomew's Day Massacre
Feb. 1576	Henry of Navarre escapes from the royal court
Sept. 9, 1585	Excommunicated by Pope Sixtus V
1586	War of the three Henrys begins
Oct. 20, 1587	Henry of Navarre's forces victorious at the battle of Coutras
May 13, 1588	Henry III flees Paris
Dec. 23, 1588	Henry III murders the Duke of Guise
Jan. 5, 1589	Catherine de Médicis dies
Aug. 2, 1589	Henry III dies from wounds inflicted by an assassin
Aug. 20, 1589	Henry of Navarre becomes king of France
July 25, 1593	Converts to Catholicism
Feb. 27, 1594	Coronation (becomes Henry IV)
March 22, 1594	Takes over Paris without bloodshed
Jan. 17, 1595	Declares war against Spain
April 13, 1598	Issues the Edict of Nantes
May 2, 1598	War with Spain ends
May 14, 1610	Henry IV is murdered

Index

Albert C. Gross received his B.A. in history from Columbia University, New York City, and his M.A. in psychology from the University of California, San Diego. A psychology instructor since 1975, Gross is the author of numerous books and articles. His work has appeared in *Scientific American* and *Technology Review*, among other publications. An avid bicyclist, he has also written extensively on sports topics.

Arthur M. Schlesinger, jr., taught history at Harvard for many years and is currently Albert Schweitzer Professor of the Humanities at City University of New York. He is the author of numerous highly praised works in American history and has twice been awarded the Pulitzer Prize. He served in the White House as special assistant to Presidents Kennedy and Johnson.

PICTURE CREDITS

The Bettmann Archive: pp. 16, 22, 23, 24, 26, 29, 30, 31, 34, 35, 38, 43, 44, 45, 46, 50, 52, 54, 55, 60, 61, 62, 64, 65, 68, 70, 74, 75, 78, 88, 93, 96, 97, 98, 102, 103, 104, 105; Bibliotheque Nationale: pp. 36, 37, 91; Culver Pictures, Inc.: pp. 18, 19, 57, 66, 67, 72, 77, 80, 81, 92, 106; Giraudon/Art Resource: pp. 12, 14, 20, 48, 49, 86, 87; Lauros-Giraudon/Art Resource: pp. 15, 40, 41; New York Public Library Picture Collection: pp. 2, 25, 32, 82, 85, 90, 94, 95, 100, 101, 107